WELCOME TO THE WORLD OF ANIMALS

Octopuses

Diane Swanson

Gareth Stevens Publishing
A WORLD ALMANAC EDUCATION GROUP COMPANY

Please visit our web site at: www.garethstevens.com
For a free color catalog describing Gareth Stevens Publishing's list of high-quality books
and multimedia programs, call 1-800-542-2595 (USA) or 1-800-387-3178 (Canada).
Gareth Stevens Publishing's fax: (414) 332-3567.

The author gratefully acknowledges Jim Cosgrove of the Royal British Columbia Museum for reviewing this manuscript.

The publishers acknowledge the support of the Canada Council for the Arts and the Cultural Services Branch of the Government of British Columbia in making this publication possible.

Library of Congress Cataloging-in-Publication Data

Swanson, Diane, 1944-
    [Welcome to the world of octopuses]
    Octopuses / by Diane Swanson. — North American ed.
      p. cm. — (Welcome to the world of animals)
    Includes index.
    Summary: Describes the physical characteristics and behavior of the octopus, the smartest of the world's spineless animals.
    ISBN 0-8368-3314-7 (lib. bdg.)
    1. Octopus—Juvenile literature. [1. Octopus.] I. Title.
QL430.3.O2S9   2002
594'.56—dc21   2002021107

This edition first published in 2002 by
Gareth Stevens Publishing
A World Almanac Education Group Company
330 West Olive Street, Suite 100
Milwaukee, WI 53212 USA

This U.S. edition © 2002 by Gareth Stevens, Inc. Original edition © 2000 by Diane Swanson. First published in 2000 by Whitecap Books, Vancouver/Toronto. Additional end matter © 2002 by Gareth Stevens, Inc.

Series editor: Patricia Lantier
Design: Katherine A. Goedheer
Cover design: Renee M. Bach

Cover photograph: James B. Wood
Photo credits: James A. Cosgrove 4, 8, 14, 16, 18, 22, 30; David Doubilet/First Light 6; George Grall/First Light 10; Neil G. McDaniel 12; James B. Wood 20, 26; David Hamilton 24; Seattle Aquarium 28

Printed in the United States of America

1 2 3 4 5 6 7 8 9 06 05 04 03 02

Contents

World of Difference

An octopus is mostly arms — and what wonderful arms they are! All eight of them can stretch, twist, and bend without having any joints. Along these arms sit rows of suckers — dozens or even hundreds, depending on the age and kind of octopus. These suckers work independently, gripping objects such as small stones and fine wires.

The octopus has a soft body with no bones. It doesn't even have a shell, although its ancestors once did. Its only hard part, a strong parrotlike beak, is surrounded by its eight arms.

The giant Pacific octopus is one kind of cold-sea octopus that might live over four years.

The headlike mantle of the octopus is a bag of skin and muscle that keeps the brain and other organs under cover. The mantle also contains glands that secrete slime onto its skin. Wearing a slimy coat protects an octopus from infection and helps it slide easily through small openings.

No one knows how many different kinds of octopuses exist, but at least sixty kinds live around North America.

As an octopus swims, it shoots water out of the short, hoselike funnel above its arms.

Worldwide, there are probably over 150 kinds of octopuses. Some are shorter than a paper clip, but others stretch the length of three doors or more.

An octopus has no ears, so it depends on other sense organs. Its arms — especially its suckers — are used for touching, smelling, and tasting. Its eyes can see as well as yours. Peeking over rocks is easy for an octopus because it can raise its eyes above its mantle.

MOVING RIGHT ALONG

Reach, anchor, and p-u-l-l. Using all the suckers on its long arms, an octopus crawls quickly and effortlessly across the seafloor.

When it swims, the octopus sucks water into its mantle and fires it out through its funnel. Then the octopus jets backward, its eight arms trailing behind. It can easily shift direction by pointing its funnel different ways. If it wants to swim slowly, the octopus simply squirts out water with much less force.

Where in the World

Octopuses hang out in salty seas. Some live in tide pools or in shallow water close to shore. Others stay in deep water — more than 2 miles (3 kilometers) down. There they feel and smell their way through the dark. Some kinds of octopuses range between shallow and deep water.

When an octopus is not out searching for food, it's usually snuggling inside one of its dens. Caves or holes in undersea rocks, and nooks and crannies in sunken ships, make good octopus homes. So do roomy shells and castoff pails and cans. Sometimes an octopus builds a den out of piles of

Luckily for this octopus, it found a hiding place beneath a rocky outcrop.

9

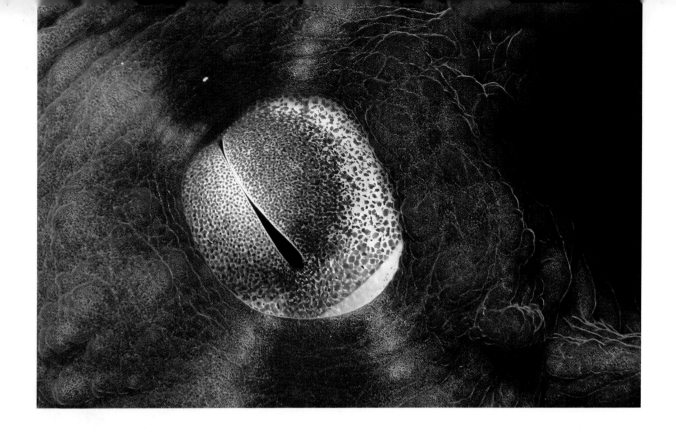

An octopus views its world through narrow slits — its pupils.

stones, shells, and bottle caps. Or it might use these items to narrow or hide the entrance to its den.

Even a large octopus needs only a small doorway. Its soft body can squeeze through almost any opening wide enough for its beak.

An octopus lives all on its own, but it often has several dens. It might use one at each end of its hunting range and others in between for protection while eating. Some dens are used again and again by generations of octopuses; others are used only once.

Nearly every ocean in the world is home to some kinds of octopuses, but warm waters have a larger variety. Off the coasts of North America, octopuses live in the Pacific Ocean, Atlantic Ocean, and Gulf of Mexico.

OCTO-WATCH

It's not easy to watch an octopus. It tends to watch right back — and it usually tries to hide. Besides, divers aren't able to stay underwater for long periods of time.

Researchers sometimes attach a special tag to an octopus so they can track its movements by radio from a boat or satellite. Or they might use a camera on an ROV (Remotely Operated Vehicle) to follow an octopus day and night. Once it gets used to the camera, the octopus doesn't seem bothered by it.

World Full of Food

Crabs, scallops, snails, fish — they're just some of the animals an octopus eats. Like you, it dines on its favorite foods, but a big octopus might also grab seabirds — or even smaller octopuses — if it has a chance.

When it spies lunch, an octopus sneaks in close. Then it leaps. The octopus traps its prey in a pocket of water under its webbed arms. Next, it releases a toxin from its glands into the pocket, stunning its victim.

Sometimes an octopus pokes the tips of its arms into cracks and holes — sniffing, tasting, and feeling for food. When it finds something good to eat, the octopus yanks

Working its way across the seafloor, an octopus is on the hunt.

A pile of shells, mostly from crabs, is all that remains of an octopus feast.

the prey out, stuns it, and tucks it under its arms. Before heading back to its den to eat, the octopus might gather a dozen or more crabs or other small prey.

Safe at home, the octopus can use its tough beak to rip into the prey, biting or tearing off chunks of food. It can also scrape its food, using a tongue covered with thousands of tiny, horny teeth. This tongue is always replacing old worn teeth with new sharp ones.

The octopus also uses its toothy tongue to drill a hole through the thick shells of animals such as clams. It injects chemicals that turn the animals' soft insides to mush, then it sucks or scrapes them out with its tongue. Leftovers are pushed outside the den. A growing pile of empty shells can show divers the location of an octopus hideout.

GONE FISHING

It can be hard to keep an octopus at home. One aquarium store owner discovered that his octopus gobbled up some of his fish at night. Alone in the store, it climbed out of its tank and entered the tanks of its neighbors. The octopus usually sneaked back before morning, but sometimes it hid in other parts of the store.

A big octopus might even be able to escape from a covered tank. It can raise a lid weighed down by several large cinder blocks.

World of Words

The silent octopus communicates, or "talks," with its skin. It might say "I'm mad" by raising the skin above its eyes to make a pair of "horns." Most often, an octopus speaks by changing color. Its skin has stretchy cells, each filled with a colored chemical that may be red, orange, yellow, or black. The octopus widens or narrows the openings in these cells, exposing more or less of each color. It can even display different combinations of colors.

Many kinds of octopuses can make patterns — including streaks, stripes, and blotches — on different parts of their

This ruby octopus is saying something in body language, but scientists aren't sure just what.

"Horns" of skin rising on this octopus show that it is angry.

bodies. Several also have layers of cells that reflect the colors of nearby objects.

Before male octopuses mate, they often change colors, sometimes producing stripes. That's how they tell other males to get lost. By turning a pale gray or white, many octopuses show they're frightened. A dark red might mean they're angry or excited.

Skin colors and their meanings vary with the kind of octopus. Some kinds might say "I'm content" through a patchwork of soft colors; others, by turning a dark red.

All octopuses can communicate quickly. In fact, few other animals can change color so fast. Octopuses take just a fraction of a second to open or close their color cells completely. They can run through a number of different combinations and patterns so fast that the human eye can barely follow.

OCTOPUS PUZZLE

There's a mystery about the octopus. It changes color to communicate — and to blend with its surroundings — but it can't see in color.

That doesn't matter to the skin cells that reflect colors of objects the octopus passes. And that doesn't affect the thin skin of small octopuses that lets colors show right through. But most of the octopus's amazing shades and patterns are controlled by nerves from its brain — and these nerves are triggered by what the octopus sees!

19

Dangerous World

Plenty of predators eat octopus meat. People, dolphins, seals, sea lions — even fish, such as halibut and cod — all hunt octopuses. It's a good thing these eight-armed sea creatures have several escape tricks.

Frightened by the sight of a large predator — or a boat — an octopus might try to surprise its enemy. It might suddenly change color, flatten its body, and curl its arms in toward its mantle. Some octopuses also develop dark circles around their eyes.

Then the octopus will likely shoot ink and mucus into the water. All octopuses

The color and pose of this white-spotted octopus might scare away its enemies.

Firing brown ink into the sea helps this little octopus escape from a diver.

have glands that produce dark brown or black ink. (At one time, people used it for writing.) When the ink mixes with the water, it makes a dark cloud that confuses predators. Like a screen, the ink can hide the octopus for a few seconds, and it might dull an enemy's sense of smell. If once isn't enough, some octopuses can fire ink as many as six times in a minute.

Once predators lose track of the octopus, it has a chance to jet away, firing water forcefully out of its funnel. As it swims, it quickly changes the colors and textures of its skin, blending with its surroundings.

The octopus swims until it finds a safe hiding place. Then it squeezes through a crack in rocks or swoops into a small den to take cover. Some small octopuses might hide under the sand on the seafloor.

UNARMING AN OCTOPUS

Half out of the water, an octopus clings tightly to a rock. A large bald eagle is trying to yank it off. Tugging at one arm, the eagle skillfully avoids the grasp of the octopus. After a ten-minute battle, the bird leaves to find easier prey.

Like the eagle, other predators may try to rip an arm off an octopus. Luckily, that's something the octopus can lose without dying. In fact, it can grow a whole new arm, which might even branch into several small arms at its tip!

New World

Many octopuses make good mothers. A female searches for a safe den to use as a nursery. She might even close off the entrance by building a stone wall. Then she gets busy laying her eggs — from hundreds to more than a hundred thousand of them. The eggs have already been fertilized by a male octopus. With the help of a specially designed arm, the male placed a package of sperm into the female's mantle.

Using her own mucus, the mother sticks the eggs in strands to the wall or ceiling of her den. Then she nestles close to them, where she stays day and night. She

Mom on guard! Protecting her eggs is a full-time job for this octopus.

25

See-through eggs make it possible to spot these tiny octopuses before they hatch.

rarely — if ever — eats while she guards her eggs. The octopus pushes away intruders, such as snails, sea stars, crabs, and fish, which might eat her brood. To provide the eggs with oxygen, she sprays them with water from her funnel.

In cold waters, a mother's care can continue for over six months. In warm seas, young octopuses often burst out of their eggs much sooner. As they hatch, their mother showers them with water, which helps them jiggle free of the eggs.

The new arrivals look just like tiny adult octopuses. They can change color, produce ink, and shoot water from their funnels. Predators gobble up most of the hatchlings right away. Some of the survivors — depending on the kind of octopus — drift and feed at the water's surface before heading for the seafloor.

No wonder octopuses surprise people. They do the most amazing things!

- "Armstrong" would be a good name for an octopus. It can move objects heavier than itself.

- Of all the spineless animals in the world, the octopus is the brainiest. It's about as smart as a cat.

- An octopus has three hearts — two to pump blood through its gills and one to pump blood around its body.

Fun World

It takes brains to have fun. Like cats and dogs, an octopus seems to be smart enough to play. After all, it can figure out how to get a crab out of a jar — even if it has never seen a jar before. The octopus might first try to grab the crab through the glass. But soon, it figures out how to unscrew the lid or pull out the cork to reach its prey. If another octopus is nearby, it can learn to do the same thing more easily, just by watching the first octopus.

In experiments, octopuses have learned to pick out objects of different shapes and sizes. When they are rewarded with food

What a ball! An octopus checks out new objects and seems to play with some of them.

29

for some choices and punished with mild electric shocks for others, they learn quickly. The octopuses remember their lessons quite well, too. They get better and faster with practice.

No one knows what games an octopus plays in the wild, but in an aquarium, it seems to have fun with a toy. When researchers dropped an empty pill bottle into a tank, the

Divers might all look the same to you, but an octopus can learn to tell them apart.

octopuses tasted it — in case it was food. Then some of them ignored the bottle, while others used it to play games. Squirting water from their funnels, they moved it along to the rear of the tank. A current carried it back, and they squirted the bottle away again. One octopus made the bottle circle the tank over and over. The games lasted from ten to thirty minutes. What seemed odd was that no octopus used any of its amazing arms to bat the bottle around.

GETTING TO KNOW YOU

An octopus can have fun with people. In an aquarium, it might squirt water at a familiar face or climb to the top of its tank to "greet" someone. Even in the sea, an octopus easily recognizes people it knows — in spite of their masks and all the other diving gear they wear.

Touch an octopus's arm and that arm might touch you right back. As it feels around, its strong suckers might nuzzle your fingers. They can sometimes pull a watch or ring right off!

31

Glossary

brood — (n) all the young from the same mother hatched or born at one time.

cell — the smallest unit in the body of a plant or animal that can function on its own.

gland — a part of the body that produces fluid from materials in the bloodstream.

jet — (v) to move or shoot forward in a stream of water or air.

mantle — the baglike part of an octopus made of skin and muscle.

mucus — a slimy, protective substance produced by the body.

nursery — a place where eggs or young animals are cared for.

predators — animals that hunt other animals for food.

prey — animals that are hunted by other animals for food.

secrete — to make and give off something, such as a toxin.

toxin — a poison produced by an animal or plant.

Index

ELECTRICITY
AND
MAGNETISM

M c G R A W - H I L L

SCIENCE

MACMILLAN/McGRAW-HILL EDITION

ELECTRICITY AND MAGNETISM

RICHARD MOYER ■ LUCY DANIEL ■ JAY HACKETT

PRENTICE BAPTISTE ■ PAMELA STRYKER ■ JOANNE VASQUEZ

NATIONAL
GEOGRAPHIC
SOCIETY

**McGraw-Hill
School Division**

New York   Farmington

PROGRAM AUTHORS

Dr. Lucy H. Daniel
*Teacher, Consultant
Rutherford County Schools,
North Carolina*

Dr. Jay Hackett
*Emeritus Professor of Earth
Sciences
University of Northern
Colorado*

Dr. Richard H. Moyer
*Professor of Science
Education
University of Michigan-
Dearborn*

Dr. H. Prentice Baptiste
*Professor of Curriculum and
Instruction
New Mexico State
University*

Pamela Stryker, M.Ed.
*Elementary Educator and
Science Consultant
Eanes Independent School
District
Austin, Texas*

JoAnne Vasquez, M.Ed.
*Elementary Science
Education Specialist
Mesa Public Schools,
Arizona
NSTA President 1996–1997*

NATIONAL
GEOGRAPHIC
SOCIETY

Washington, D.C.

CONTRIBUTING AUTHORS

Dr. Thomas Custer

Dr. James Flood

Dr. Diane Lapp

Doug Llewellyn

Dorothy Reid

Dr. Donald M. Silver

CONSULTANTS

Dr. Danny J. Ballard

Dr. Carol Baskin

Dr. Bonnie Buratti

Dr. Suellen Cabe

Dr. Shawn Carlson

Dr. Thomas A. Davies

Dr. Marie DiBerardino

Dr. R. E. Duhrkopf

Dr. Ed Geary

Dr. Susan C. Giarratano-Russell

Dr. Karen Kwitter

Dr. Donna Lloyd-Kolkin

Ericka Lochner, RN

Donna Harrell Lubcker

Dr. Dennis L. Nelson

Dr. Fred S. Sack

Dr. Martin VanDyke

Dr. E. Peter Volpe

Dr. Josephine Davis Wallace

Dr. Joe Yelderman

Invitation to Science, *World of Science*, and *FUNtastic Facts* features found in this textbook were designed and developed by the National Geographic Society's Education Division.

Copyright © 2000 National Geographic Society

The name "National Geographic Society" and the Yellow Border Rectangle are trademarks of the Society, and their use, without prior written permission, is strictly prohibited.

Cover Photo: *bkgnd.* PhotoDisc; *inset* PhotoDisc

RFB&D
learning through listening

Students with print disabilities may be eligible to obtain an accessible, audio version of the pupil edition of this textbook. Please call Recording for the Blind & Dyslexic at 1-800-221-4792 for complete information.

McGraw-Hill School Division
A Division of The McGraw-Hill Companies

Published by Macmillan/McGraw-Hill, a division of The McGraw-Hill Companies, Inc., Two Penn Plaza, NY, NY 10121

Printed in the United States of America

ISBN 0-02-278219-2 / 4

6 7 8 9 10 058/046 10 09 08 07 06

CONTENTS

REFERENCE SECTION

UNIT 5

ELECTRICITY AND MAGNETISM

CHAPTER 9
PATHS FOR ELECTRICITY

Electricity. Everyone knows what it does. Flip a switch—a light comes on. Flip another—a computer turns on. Electricity runs the appliances in your home. It runs the traffic lights that let you cross a street safely. It even runs some new cars! Yet few people can tell you what electricity is or how it gets from one place to another. In this chapter you will learn about what electricity is and the paths it travels to get to you.

 In this chapter you will have many opportunities to read diagrams for information.

Topic
PHYSICAL SCIENCE
1

WHY IT MATTERS

A balloon can stick to a wall for the same reason that lightning hits the ground.

SCIENCE WORDS

static electricity a buildup of electrical charge

discharge when a buildup of electrical charge empties into something

conductor a material through which electricity flows easily

insulator a material through which electricity does not flow

It's Shocking!

Have you ever been "zapped"? You pull off a sock that got stuck to a sweater in your gym bag and—zap!—you hear a loud crackling sound. You rub a balloon on a sweater and—zap!—the balloon sticks to the wall. What do you think is going on? The answer may shock you.

EXPLORE

HYPOTHESIZE What do you think will happen when two rubbed balloons are brought next to each other? Will they pull together or push apart? Write a hypothesis in your *Science Journal.*

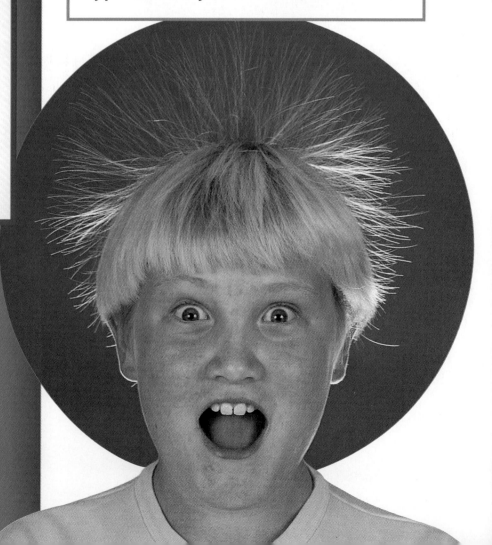

Investigate What Happens to Rubbed Balloons

Test what happens when two rubbed balloons are brought next to each other.

PROCEDURES

1. OBSERVE What happens to the balloons when you hang them as shown in the picture? Write about it in your *Science Journal*.

2. PREDICT What will happen if you rub one balloon with a piece of wool? Both balloons? Test your predictions.

3. PREDICT What will happen if you hold the wool cloth between the balloons? Test your prediction.

4. PREDICT What will happen if you put your hand between the two balloons? Test your prediction.

CONCLUDE AND APPLY

1. COMMUNICATE What happened when you rubbed one balloon with the wool cloth? Both balloons?

2. COMMUNICATE What happened when you put the wool cloth between the balloons?

3. COMMUNICATE What happened when you placed your hand between the balloons?

GOING FURTHER: Apply

4. EXPERIMENT Untie one balloon. Rub it with the wool. Try to stick the balloon to the wall. What happens? Why do you think this happened?

MATERIALS

- two 9-in.-round balloons, inflated
- 2 pieces of string, 50 cm each
- tape
- wool cloth scrap or old wool sock
- *Science Journal*

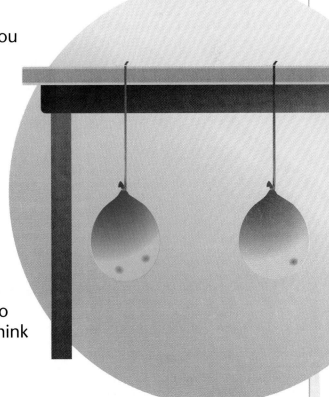

What Is Electricity?

You are probably familiar with electricity. It makes your toaster hot and your refrigerator cold. It runs through wires that you plug into the wall. However, electricity also affects things without wires—things like balloons and like socks in your gym bag. What exactly is electricity?

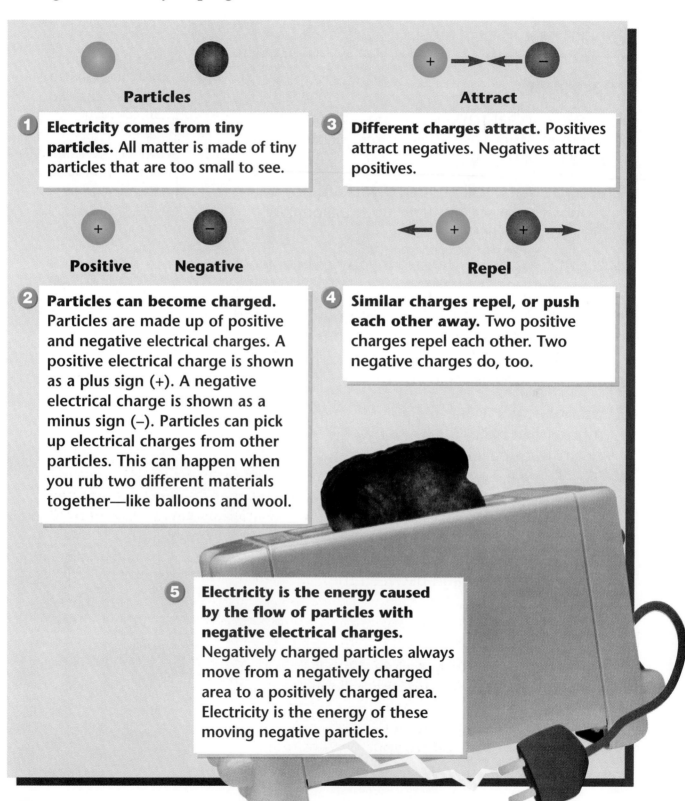

Particles

1 **Electricity comes from tiny particles.** All matter is made of tiny particles that are too small to see.

Positive   **Negative**

2 **Particles can become charged.** Particles are made up of positive and negative electrical charges. A positive electrical charge is shown as a plus sign (+). A negative electrical charge is shown as a minus sign (–). Particles can pick up electrical charges from other particles. This can happen when you rub two different materials together—like balloons and wool.

Attract

3 **Different charges attract.** Positives attract negatives. Negatives attract positives.

Repel

4 **Similar charges repel, or push each other away.** Two positive charges repel each other. Two negative charges do, too.

5 **Electricity is the energy caused by the flow of particles with negative electrical charges.** Negatively charged particles always move from a negatively charged area to a positively charged area. Electricity is the energy of these moving negative particles.

What Happens to Rubbed Balloons?

What do you think electrical charges and electricity have to do with what happened to the balloons in the Explore Activity? This diagram will help you understand why the balloons behaved as they did.

ATTRACT AND REPEL

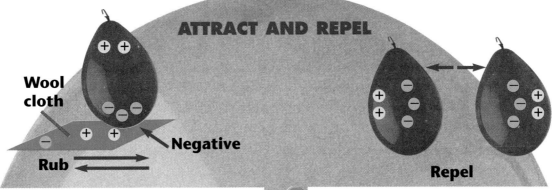

Wool cloth

Negative

Rub

Repel

1 Rubbing the balloon knocks negative charges off the cloth. These negative charges collect on the balloon and make it negative.

3 The balloon repels other negative things, such as another rubbed balloon.

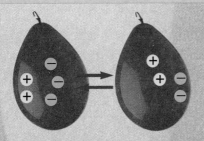

Attract

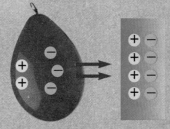

Attract

2 Now the balloon is attracted to more positively charged things, such as an unrubbed balloon.

4 The balloon's negative charges repel negative charges on the wall. This leaves a row of positive charges on the outside edge of the wall. The negatively charged balloon is attracted to the wall's positive charges and sticks to it.

READING 📊 DIAGRAMS

1. **DISCUSS** How does rubbing a balloon with a wool cloth affect the charge of the balloon?
2. **REPRESENT** Why does a rubbed balloon stick to a wall? Draw your own model.

Testing How Long Charges Last

HYPOTHESIZE Dylan plans to rub balloons and stick them to the wall for his 2-hour party. Will they stay up? Write a hypothesis in your *Science Journal.*

Come to a Party!

MATERIALS

- 3-in. balloon, inflated
- clock or watch
- *Science Journal*

PROCEDURES

1. Rub the balloon on your shirt or hair. Stick it to the wall.

2. Time how long it takes the balloon to fall. Record the time in your *Science Journal.*

CONCLUDE AND APPLY

1. **OBSERVE** How long did the balloon stay on the wall?

2. **INTERPRET DATA** Does the electrical charge last long enough to hold the balloons up for Dylan's entire party? Explain.

3. **INFER** Why do you think the balloons fell?

Why Do Balloons Fall from the Wall?

To answer this question, you need to know about the type of electricity that causes the balloons to stick. It is called **static electricity** (stat′ik i lek tris′i tē).

Static electricity is a buildup of electric charge. When the buildup of negative charge on a balloon becomes strong enough, it will attract the positively charged particles in a wall. Soon charges on the balloon "leak" away. That is why Dylan's party balloons eventually will fall.

1

A negatively charged balloon sticks to a wall.

2

With time, negative charges leak away from the balloon.

3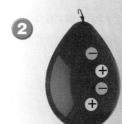

Then the balloon is no longer attracted to the wall. It falls away.

What Other Things Happen to Charges?

The Quick Lab activity showed evidence that charges move between objects. Electrical charges can also travel through certain materials. When you walk on a rug, static electricity builds up on your shoes. The charge keeps building until you touch something. Then—zap! It suddenly empties, or **discharges** (dis chärj′əz), into the object. You might feel this discharge as a small shock. The shocks you often feel when you touch objects like doorknobs, water fountains, and even other people are all small discharges.

Static electricity doesn't discharge into all types of materials. "Why not?" you might wonder. The answer is that electricity flows where it can. It flows easily through materials called **conductors** (kən duk′tərz). An **insulator** (in′sə lā′tər) is a material through which electricity does not flow.

What types of materials do you think are good conductors? Metal is a very good conductor. That is why you might feel a shock when you touch a metal doorknob. The static electricity on your shoes travels through your body to your hand. When your hand gets near the metal knob—zap! The charges jump the gap, and you feel a shock.

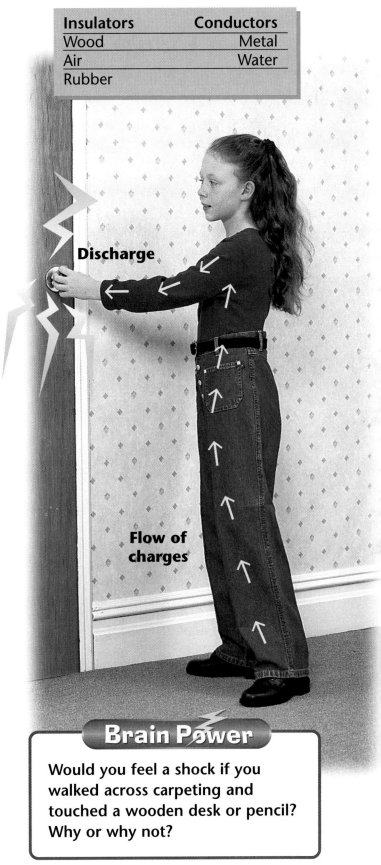

Insulators	Conductors
Wood	Metal
Air	Water
Rubber	

Discharge

Flow of charges

Brain Power

Would you feel a shock if you walked across carpeting and touched a wooden desk or pencil? Why or why not?

How Does Lightning Form?

How big can a static electricity buildup get? It can form a lightning bolt! *Lightning* (lit′ning) is a discharge of static electricity from a huge cloud called a thundercloud. It is no different from the zap you get from touching a doorknob—just bigger. A single lightning bolt has enough power to light 100 million light bulbs!

LIGHTNING

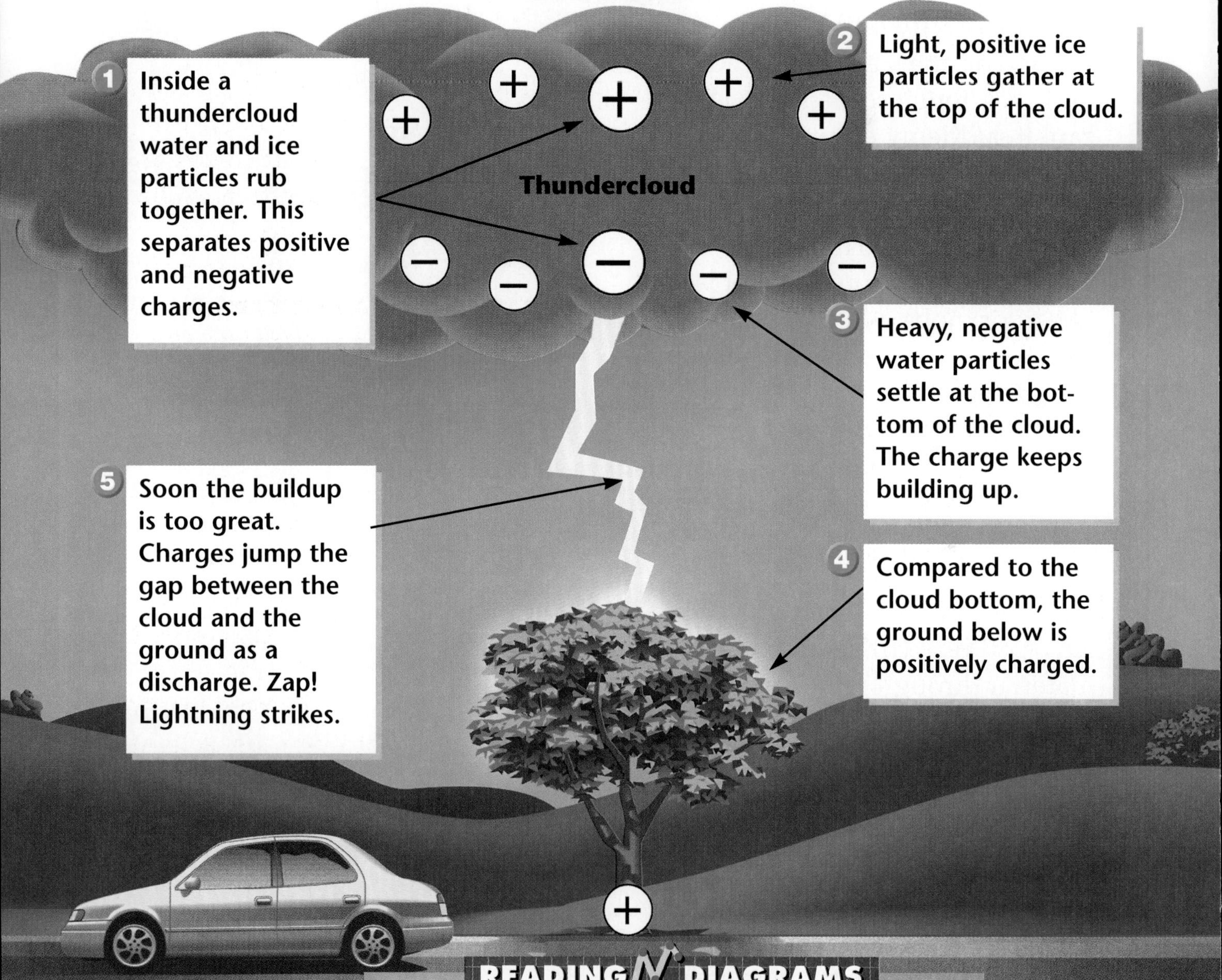

1 Inside a thundercloud water and ice particles rub together. This separates positive and negative charges.

2 Light, positive ice particles gather at the top of the cloud.

Thundercloud

3 Heavy, negative water particles settle at the bottom of the cloud. The charge keeps building up.

5 Soon the buildup is too great. Charges jump the gap between the cloud and the ground as a discharge. Zap! Lightning strikes.

4 Compared to the cloud bottom, the ground below is positively charged.

READING DIAGRAMS

1. **DISCUSS** What causes positive and negative charges to separate within a thundercloud?
2. **REPRESENT** Where do negative charges build up in a cloud? Draw a picture.

Where Does Lightning Go?

Sometimes lightning bolts occur inside the thundercloud and never leave it. Sometimes lightning bolts occur between two clouds. Other times lightning strikes the ground or objects on the ground.

Lightning gives off energy in several forms. One form is light energy. Another form is heat energy. You can see evidence of heat energy in burn marks on a struck tree. A third form is sound energy. You hear this as thunder. Some electrical energy can also travel through a struck object. This energy moves into the ground, or is grounded.

Why does lightning strike some places and not others? Lightning targets the clearest, shortest path to the ground. That may be through a tall tree or building. Lightning also targets the best conductor.

That is why people often use lightning rods. A lightning rod safely discharges lightning into the ground. A lightning rod is made of metal. It is usually placed at the very top of a building. A wire connects the lightning rod to the ground. When lightning strikes the rod, the electrical energy flows through the wire and into the ground.

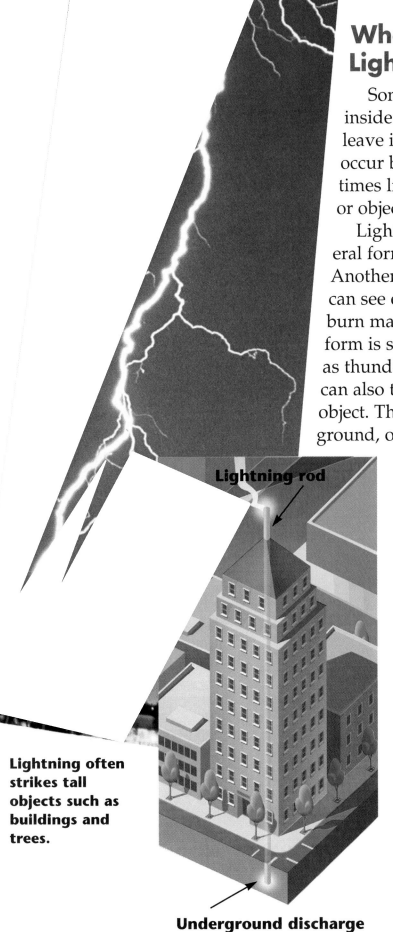

Lightning rod

Lightning often strikes tall objects such as buildings and trees.

Underground discharge

How Do You Keep Safe from Lightning?

Lightning is a very dangerous discharge of static electricity. You should always take lightning very seriously. Getting struck by lightning can cause severe injuries and even death. Understanding how lightning behaves can help keep you safe. Following these simple rules can keep you safe, too.

LIGHTNING DOS AND DON'TS

HEALTH LINK

If you hear thunder, or see or suspect lightning:

1. Stay away from high places, like the top of a hill.

2. Stay away from trees and other tall objects.

3. Crouch down if you feel your hair stand on end.

4. Get out of the water.

5. Don't use the telephone.

6. If you are in a car, stay inside. Close the windows and doors.

7. Don't touch electrical devices or anything made of metal.

READING DIAGRAMS

1. **WRITE** Make a list of lightning "dos and don'ts" for your home.
2. **DISCUSS** Why do you think you should not touch anything made of metal during a lightning storm?

WHY IT MATTERS

About 2,600 years ago, the ancient Greeks noticed the effects of static electricity when they rubbed fur on amber, which is hardened tree sap. They named the force they felt after *elektron*, their word for amber. Today our understanding of static electricity has come a long way.

Knowing what static electricity is and how it is formed explains what causes shocks to be felt and balloons to stick to walls. Understanding shocks and lightning allows you to keep safe.

Lightning is a dangerous form of static electricity.

REVIEW

1. Why does a rubbed balloon stick to the wall?

2. You rub two balloons on the same cloth. Explain what happens when you bring them close together. Draw a diagram.

3. How is lightning formed? What are some things you can do to keep safe from lightning?

4. **DRAW CONCLUSIONS** Balloon A was rubbed with a wool cloth. Balloon B was rubbed with plastic wrap. The balloons attracted each other. Did the plastic wrap make balloon B positive or negative? How did it do that?

5. **CRITICAL THINKING** *Analyze* Would a wooden lightning rod work? Why or why not?

WHY IT MATTERS THINK ABOUT IT Why do you think the ancient Greeks might have first started thinking about static electricity?

WHY IT MATTERS WRITE ABOUT IT The ancient Greeks made static electricity by rubbing fur on amber. Explain how this created static electricity.

World of SCIENCE

A SHOCKING Story

Franklin built little devices to use in his experiments.

History of Science

Benjamin Franklin was a leader of the young United States. He was also a scientist.

In 1746 Franklin began to experiment with electricity. He believed electricity was a fluid. He thought that objects with lots of it had a positive charge. He thought that electricity jumped from them to objects with less of it—those with a negative charge.

Franklin found that electricity jumped quickly to a sharp, pointed object. It jumped more slowly to an object that wasn't pointed. He also noted that electricity was like lightning. Both were the same color, made the same noise, and could destroy things!

Franklin suggested some experiments to find out if lightning was electricity. However, he didn't do them right away. He was waiting for the construction of a church steeple with a sharp point. Franklin hoped the steeple would attract lightning from the clouds.

In 1752 Franklin decided not to wait any longer. He tied a key to a kite string and flew the kite in a storm. Suddenly threads on the string stuck straight out. A spark jumped from the key to Franklin's knuckle! Luckily Franklin let go of the string before he was killed.

Thanks to Franklin we now know that lightning is static electricity. We also have the lightning rod!

Franklin's most famous experiment was a shocker!

Discussion
Starter

1 Why did threads on the kite string stick out?

2 Why was the kite experiment so dangerous?

*inter*NET
CONNECTION To learn more about Benjamin Franklin, visit www.mhschool.com/science and enter the keyword FRANKLIN.

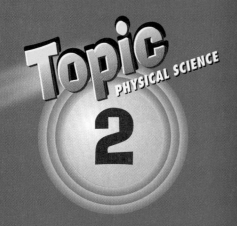

Topic 2
PHYSICAL SCIENCE

WHY IT MATTERS

We use and depend on many electrical pathways in our daily activities.

SCIENCE WORDS

circuit a complete path that electricity can move through

current electricity a moving electrical charge

closed circuit a complete circuit

open circuit an incomplete circuit

resistor a material through which electricity has difficulty flowing

short circuit when too much current flows through a conductor

switch a device that can open or close a circuit

Electrical Pathways

Have you ever had one of those camping trips where everything went wrong? Unfortunately Corky is having one of those trips. Now something is wrong with her flashlight. She made a list of what could be wrong.

Could the problem be something else? What else might it be?

EXPLORE

HYPOTHESIZE What parts are needed to make a light bulb light? How should they be arranged? Write a hypothesis in your *Science Journal.* What kind of experiment can you design to test your ideas?

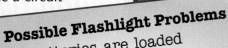

Possible Flashlight Problems
1. The batteries are loaded incorrectly.
2. The batteries are dead.
3. The bulb is no good.
4. The flashlight was damaged when it fell in muddy water.

Investigate What Makes a Bulb Light

Test what makes a bulb light by arranging the materials in different ways.

MATERIALS

- flashlight bulb
- 20 cm of wire with stripped ends
- D-cell
- cell holder
- *Science Journal*

PROCEDURES

1. **EXPERIMENT** Work with your group to try to light the bulb using the materials. Draw each setup in your *Science Journal*. Record your results.

2. **PREDICT** Study the drawings on this page. Predict in which setups the bulb will light and in which it will not light. Record your predictions.

3. **EXPERIMENT** Work with another group of students to test each setup. Can you see a pattern?

CONCLUDE AND APPLY

1. **OBSERVE** How many ways could you arrange the materials to make the bulb light in step 1?

2. **COMPARE** How were the ways to light the bulb using only one wire similar?

3. **COMPARE** How were the ways that did *not* light the bulb using only one wire similar?

4. **COMPARE** In which drawings did the bulb light? How are the setups similar?

GOING FURTHER: Problem Solving

5. **PREDICT** Draw another setup. Challenge a classmate to determine if the bulb will light.

What Makes a Bulb Light?

The Explore Activity showed a pattern in the setups that made the bulb light. All the setups that worked had one thing in common. They formed a complete path. The path went from one end of the D-cell. Then, it went through the bulb. Next, it went back to the other end of the D-cell. A complete path that electricity can move through is called a **circuit** (sûr'kit). A circuit is a system made up of many parts that work together to allow electricity to flow.

Here are four circuits that will make a bulb light using the materials from the Explore Activity. Trace the path in each.

Electricity Flow in a Circuit

The electricity that flows through a circuit is a little different from static electricity. Remember, static electricity is a buildup of electrical charge. The electricity that flows through a circuit is called **current electricity** (kûr'ənt i lek tris'i tē). Current electricity is moving electrical charge.

Can you think of something else that flows? What about a liquid, like water? Water flows in streams, rivers, pipes, and hoses. Current electricity itself is not *like* water. However, in many ways it *behaves like* flowing water. Both flow only if they have a clear path. For example, if the path of flowing water is clear, it flows freely. If the path isn't clear, it stops flowing.

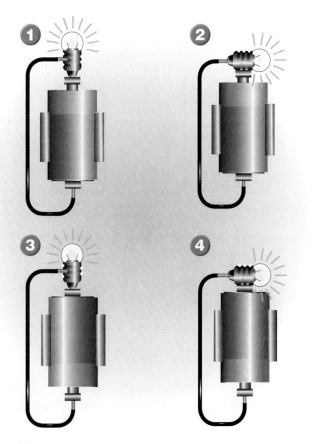

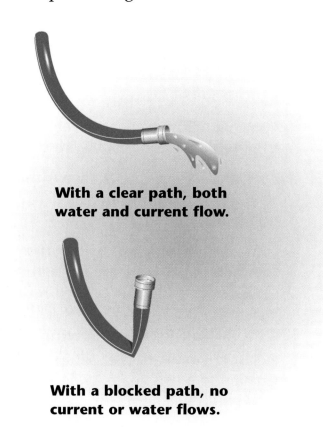

With a clear path, both water and current flow.

With a blocked path, no current or water flows.

When Will Current Flow in a Circuit?

With electric circuits a complete path is called a **closed circuit** (klōzd sûr′kit). In a closed circuit, there are no gaps or places where current cannot flow.

An incomplete path is called an **open circuit** (ō′pən sûr′kit). No current flows in an open circuit. The path is not complete. There are gaps, or places where current cannot flow. As in any system, when a part is missing, the system does not work properly.

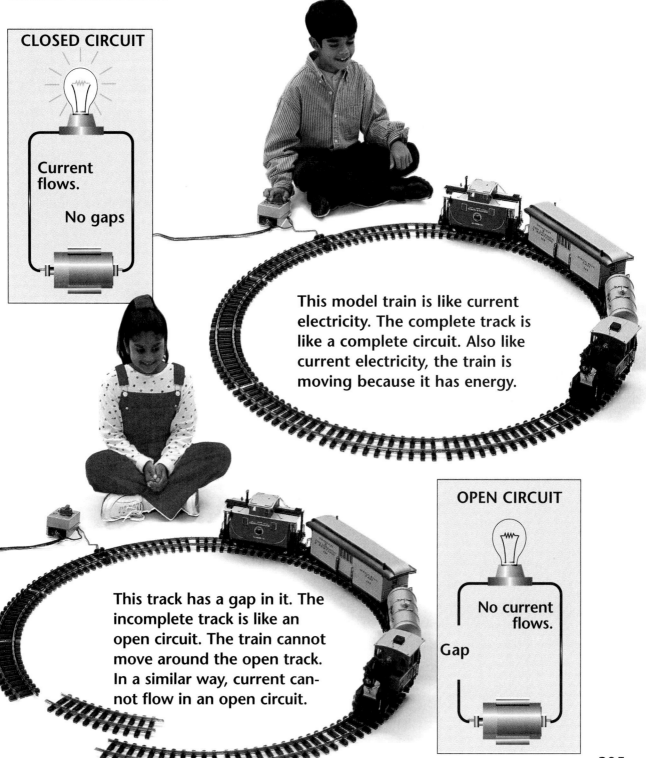

CLOSED CIRCUIT

Current flows.

No gaps

This model train is like current electricity. The complete track is like a complete circuit. Also like current electricity, the train is moving because it has energy.

This track has a gap in it. The incomplete track is like an open circuit. The train cannot move around the open track. In a similar way, current cannot flow in an open circuit.

OPEN CIRCUIT

No current flows.

Gap

Where Does Current Come From?

One way to make current is by using a cell. A cell changes chemical energy into electrical energy. A battery is made up of several connected cells. One type of cell is a wet cell. You will learn about wet cells in Topic 5. Another type of cell is a dry cell.

What parts of a dry cell can you identify in this diagram? This diagram shows what is inside one type of dry cell. Down the center is a rod made of the element carbon. Surrounding the carbon rod is a moist chemical paste. Around the paste is a container made of the element zinc. *Never* open a cell. The paste inside can harm your skin.

On the outside of the dry cell are two places where wires can be attached. These are called *terminals* (tûr′mə nəlz). The positive terminal is attached to the carbon rod. The negative terminal is attached to the zinc container.

A chemical change takes place within the cell. This makes the zinc container more negatively charged. The carbon rod becomes more positively charged. Current flows when a conductor is attached between the cell's positive and negative terminals. Remember, opposite charges attract each other. Therefore, the negative charges travel from the negative terminal, through the conductor, and on to the cell's positive terminal.

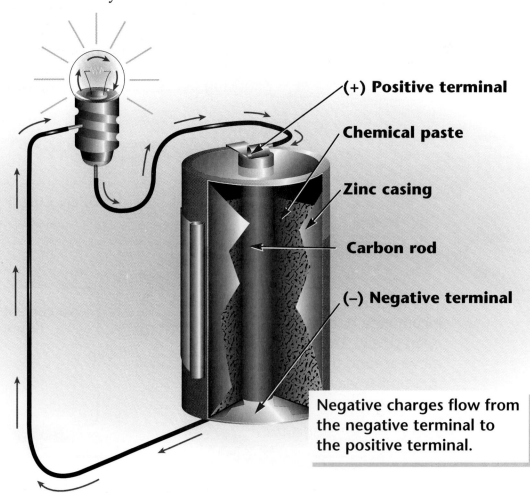

(+) Positive terminal

Chemical paste

Zinc casing

Carbon rod

(–) Negative terminal

Negative charges flow from the negative terminal to the positive terminal.

How Does a Light Bulb Work?

The circuit on page 306 includes a light bulb. Current from the dry cell lights the bulb. How do you think this happens? To understand how a light bulb works, you must first learn about its parts.

1 A light bulb is a ball of glass. Inside the bulb most of the air has been removed.

2 The bulb has a metal base that can be screwed into a socket. The metal socket is a good conductor. You remember from Topic 1 that electricity flows easily through a conductor. Electricity does not flow through an insulator.

4 Between the two wires is a thin, coiled wire. It is called a filament (fil'ə mənt). The filament, however, is a poor conductor. It is a **resistor** (ri zis'tər). Current does not flow easily through a resistor. This resistance causes the filament to get so hot that it glows. That is how the bulb creates light and heat. The air in the bulb has been removed to keep the filament from burning up.

3 Two wires extend into the bulb from the base. These wires are also good conductors.

READING N DIAGRAMS

1. **WRITE** What are the parts of a light bulb? Make a list.
2. **DISCUSS** What parts of a light bulb are good conductors?
3. **DISCUSS** Why does the bulb give off light and heat?

QUICK LAB

Conductor Test-Off

HYPOTHESIZE The base and wires of a light bulb are good conductors. The filament is a poor conductor. What other materials are good conductors or insulators? Write a hypothesis in your *Science Journal.*

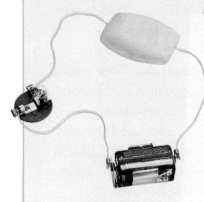

MATERIALS
- flashlight bulb
- bulb socket
- D-cell
- cell holder
- 3 wires with stripped ends, 20 cm each
- assorted test objects
- *Science Journal*

PROCEDURES

1. **EXPERIMENT** Make a circuit as shown, using one of the test objects. Record your observations in your *Science Journal.*

2. **REPEAT** Test the other objects. Record your observations.

CONCLUDE AND APPLY

1. **OBSERVE** Which objects were good conductors? Which were not? How could you tell?

2. **INFER** Examine a length of wire. Which part of the wire is a conductor? Which part is an insulator? Why do you think the wire is made this way?

What Can Go Wrong in a Circuit?

Current always follows the path with the least resistance. If at all possible, it would flow through a conductor rather than a resistor.

How does the current flow in the diagram below? In this diagram the connecting wire is a better conductor than the filament. It has less resistance than the filament. Therefore, current avoids the bulb. It takes the path with less resistance to the cell.

That causes too much current to flow through the conductors. This is called a **short circuit** (shôrt sûr′kit).

In your home a short circuit can also occur if frayed or broken wires touch. This heats up the wires and can cause a fire.

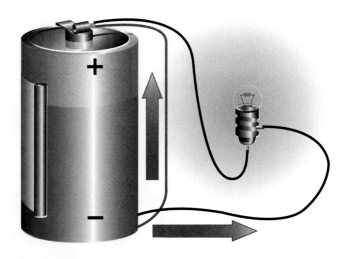

This is one example of a short circuit

How Can You Control Current in a Circuit?

This circuit is set up to make an electric door buzzer. In this system some of the electricity is transformed into sound energy. When the circuit is closed, the buzzer makes a sound.

What do you think might be wrong with the circuit in figure A? The buzzer never stops buzzing because the circuit stays closed. Figures B and C show a different setup that uses a **switch** (swich). A switch is a device that can open or close a circuit. It is used to control current in a circuit.

What do you see in figure B? Figure B shows the switch in the open position. No current flows. The buzzer doesn't buzz.

What do you see in figure C? Figure C shows what happens when you push the switch button. The circuit closes. Current flows. The buzzer buzzes. When you stop pushing the button, the switch opens again. Current stops flowing. The buzzer stops buzzing.

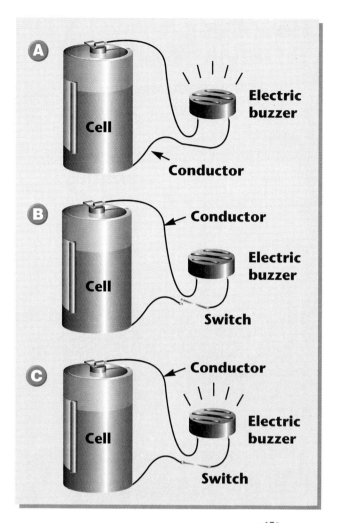

Brain Power

Somebody rang your doorbell. Now it won't stop ringing! What could be wrong?

NATIONAL GEOGRAPHIC

FUNtastic Facts

Electric eels can produce enough current to stun or even kill a human. An electric eel's body has layers of tissue, one under the other, like the plates in a car battery. Chemicals in the eel's body flow through these tissues and produce electricity. How does this feature help the eel survive?

How Does a Flashlight Work?

Now you know about all the parts Corky needs to make her flashlight work. A flashlight is a type of circuit. The circuit includes an energy supply, a conductor, a resistor, and a switch.

Look at the diagrams below. Pushing the switch back creates an open circuit. No current flows. The flashlight is off. Pushing the switch forward creates a closed circuit. Current flows from the cells to the bulb. The filament in the bulb gets very hot and glows.

Current completes the circuit by traveling through the wire to the other end of the cells. Pushing the switch back to the open position will open the circuit and turn off the flashlight.

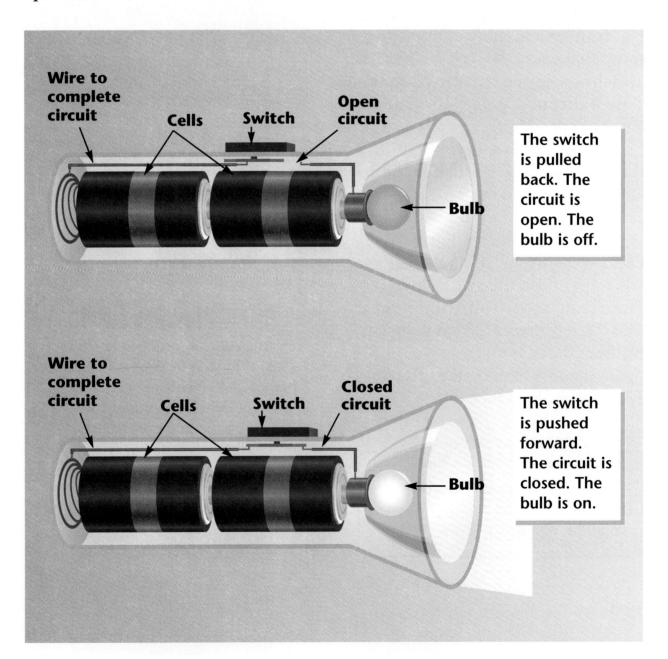

Wire to complete circuit

Cells

Switch

Open circuit

Bulb

The switch is pulled back. The circuit is open. The bulb is off.

Wire to complete circuit

Cells

Switch

Closed circuit

Bulb

The switch is pushed forward. The circuit is closed. The bulb is on.

Electricity has become an important part of our lives. As a matter of fact, almost every part of our lives depends on electricity. We use it to create light. We use it to communicate. Electricity powers machines large and small. We use it to keep our food cold and our homes warm.

Knowing how electricity travels allows us to investigate the parts of a circuit to see what is wrong when electricity doesn't flow. This is important when there is a power loss or something like a flashlight doesn't work. Electricity—imagine trying to live without it!

How many ways did you use electricity today? Keep a log.

REVIEW

1. How does a dry cell work to provide electricity?

2. What is a short circuit?

3. What does each part of a flashlight circuit do? What causes the bulb to light?

4. **INFER** Why does a radio go off when you unplug it? Explain in terms of closed and open circuits.

5. **CRITICAL THINKING** *Analyze* How could dirt inside a flashlight prevent it from working? Think of two ways.

WHY IT MATTERS THINK ABOUT IT
How would our lives be different if we did not know how to create and control electricity?

WHY IT MATTERS WRITE ABOUT IT
Write about a morning that you get up and there is no electricity. What can't you do without it? What can you do instead?

READING SKILL Use the information you find in the diagram on page 310 to describe the closed circuit that makes the bulb light.

MAKING LIGHT OF ELECTRICITY

What did people do at night before there were electric lights? Most people stopped working shortly after sunset. At night they lighted their homes with fires, candles, or gas lamps. It was too hard to sew or read by such dim light, so people went to bed!

Then came the invention of electric lights. People could do things at night that they once could do only by day. They stayed up later to visit friends, read, and sew. They slept longer in the morning because they could work later in the evening!

Some of the first electric lights were arc lights. They're created when a strong electric current jumps through the air and hits a target made of carbon. The carbon glows with a bright, white light.

Lewis H. Latimer

312

Science, Technology, and Society

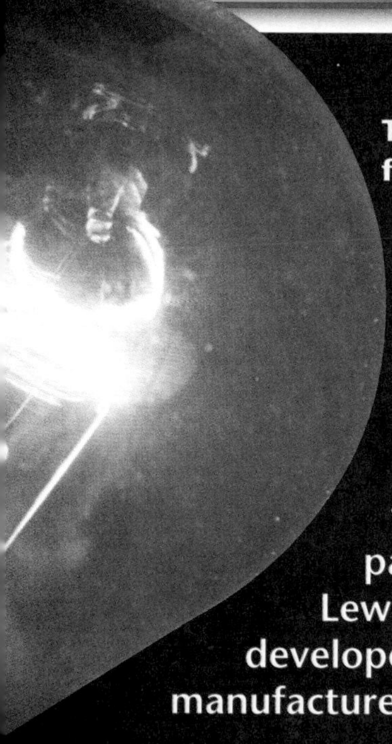

Thomas Edison's first light bulb

Inventors found that a thin wire of carbon glows when a current passes through it. Lewis H. Latimer developed the process to manufacture carbon filaments.

The first successful carbon-wire lamps were built by Thomas Edison and Joseph Swan in 1879. This event is called "the invention of the electric light." About 20 years later, a metal called tungsten (tung°stæn) was found to be the best filament. We still use tungsten-wire light bulbs today.

DISCUSSION STARTER

1. How did the way people live change as a result of the invention of electric lights?

2. How are neon lights different from other electric lights?

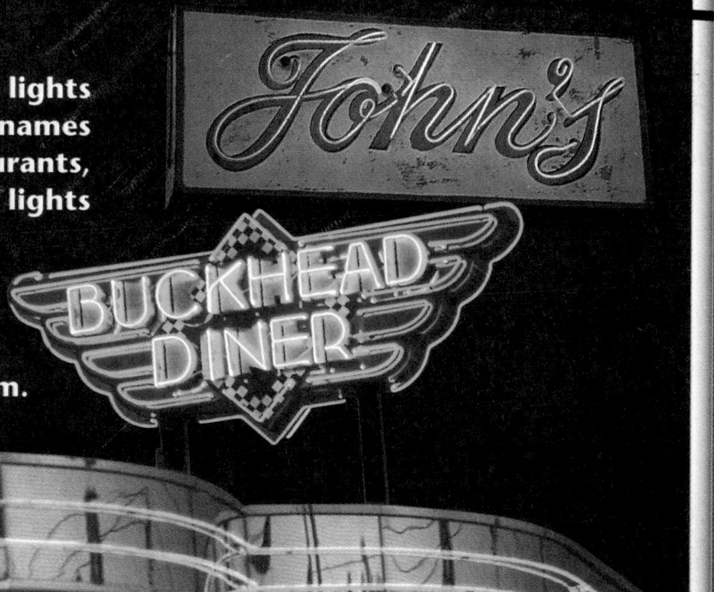

You see "neon" lights that spell out the names of theaters, restaurants, and stores. These lights contain gases, including neon, that glow when a current flows through them.

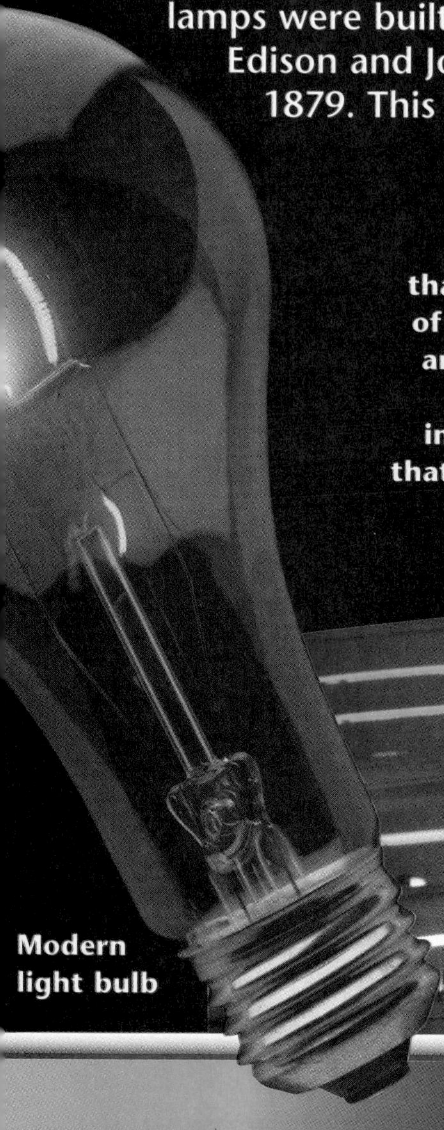

John's

BUCKHEAD DINER

To learn more about electricity, visit *www.mhschool.com/science* and enter the keyword FILAMENT.

*inter*NET
CONNECTION

Modern light bulb

313

Topic
PHYSICAL SCIENCE
3

WHY IT MATTERS

Different circuit types let you control how electricity works.

SCIENCE WORDS

series circuit a circuit in which the current must flow through one bulb in order to flow through the other

parallel circuit a circuit in which each bulb is connected to the cell separately

fuse a device that keeps too much electric current from flowing through wires

circuit breaker a switch that protects circuits from dangerously high currents

Different Circuits

What if you could use only one electrical device at a time? What if you had to turn off all the lights to iron clothes, dry your hair, or use a computer?

Luckily you can usually turn on more than one electrical device at the same time. Do you think each has its own circuit? Might they be part of the same circuit?

EXPL⊙RE

HYPOTHESIZE How can you light two bulbs with one cell? Can you have one bulb on and one bulb off? Write a hypothesis in your *Science Journal*. What kind of experiment can you design to test your ideas?

EXPLORE ACTIVITY

Investigate How to Light Two Bulbs with One Cell

Build two different circuits. Observe how electric energy interacts with the parts of a circuit to light bulbs.

MATERIALS

- D-cell
- cell holder
- 2 flashlight bulbs
- 2 bulb holders
- 4 pieces of wire with ends stripped, 20 cm each
- *Science Journal*

PROCEDURES

1. **EXPERIMENT** Build a circuit that will light two bulbs. Use one D-cell and the fewest number of wires. Draw it in your *Science Journal*. Label it Circuit 1.

2. **PREDICT** When both bulbs are lit, predict what will happen if you remove one bulb. Test your prediction. Record your results.

3. **EXPERIMENT** Construct another circuit that will light two bulbs. One bulb should remain lit if you remove the other. Draw it in your *Science Journal*. Label it Circuit 2.

4. **COMPARE** Record in which circuit the bulbs were brighter.

CONCLUDE AND APPLY

1. **INFER** Why do you think the bulbs were brighter in one circuit than the other?

2. **COMPARE AND CONTRAST** How can removing and replacing a bulb be like opening and closing a switch?

3. **DRAW CONCLUSIONS** When you removed a bulb, why did the other bulb go out in one circuit but not in the other?

GOING FURTHER: Apply

4. **INFER** What kind of circuit do you think works best in your home? Why?

315

How Can You Light Two Bulbs with One Cell?

The Explore Activity showed that each one of two different types of circuits behaved in a certain way. Now take a closer look at two different circuits to understand why.

The first type is like circuit 1 in the Explore Activity. It shows two light bulbs connected in a **series**

circuit (sîr′ēz sûr′kit). A series circuit puts both bulbs in the same circuit. The arrows show how the current flows through the parts of the circuit.

Can you think of some other things that follow one after another and are called "a series"?

When both bulbs are in place in a series circuit, it is a closed circuit. When one bulb is removed, an open

SERIES CIRCUIT

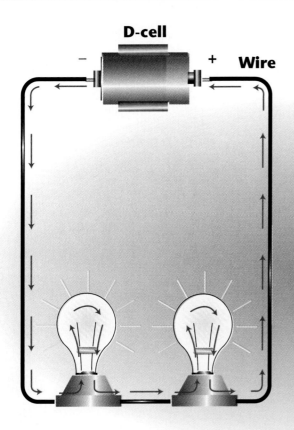

D-cell
− +
Wire

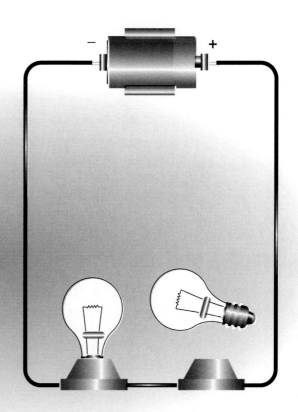

− +

	Series	Parallel
Connection	Both bulbs are on the same circuit.	Each bulb is on a separate circuit.
Removing one bulb	Both bulbs go off.	Only the removed bulb goes off.
Brightness	Dim	Bright

circuit is created. In an open circuit, current can't complete its path. The remaining bulb does not light without current flowing through its filament. A series circuit is a type of system that does not work when a part is removed.

The second type circuit is like circuit 2 in the Explore Activity. It shows two light bulbs connected in a **parallel circuit** (par′ə lel′ sûr′kit). A parallel circuit connects

each bulb to the cell separately.

When one bulb is removed from a parallel circuit, the other bulb is still a part of a complete circuit. That is why it remains lit. A parallel circuit is a type of system that still works when a part is removed because there is still a complete circuit.

The table on page 316 compares series and parallel circuits that contain two bulbs.

PARALLEL CIRCUIT

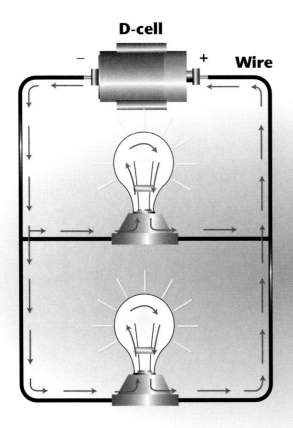

D-cell

Wire

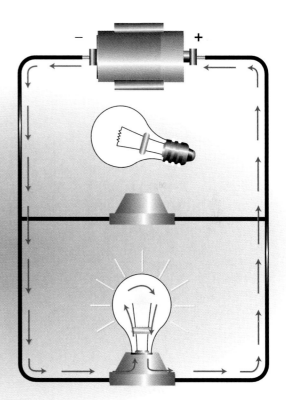

READING [N] DIAGRAMS

1. **DISCUSS** How are the series and parallel circuits on these two pages different?
2. **REPRESENT** How are the circuits similar? Make a chart.

Why Are Bulbs Brighter in a Parallel Circuit than in a Series Circuit?

Why do you think the light bulbs were brighter in the parallel circuit than in the series circuit in the Explore Activity? Comparing electric current with cars traveling along a road will help you find out.

This diagram compares a road with a series circuit. Each construction area narrowing the road acts like a resistor in a circuit. Cars traveling along this road would be slowed down as they passed each "resistor," or construction site.

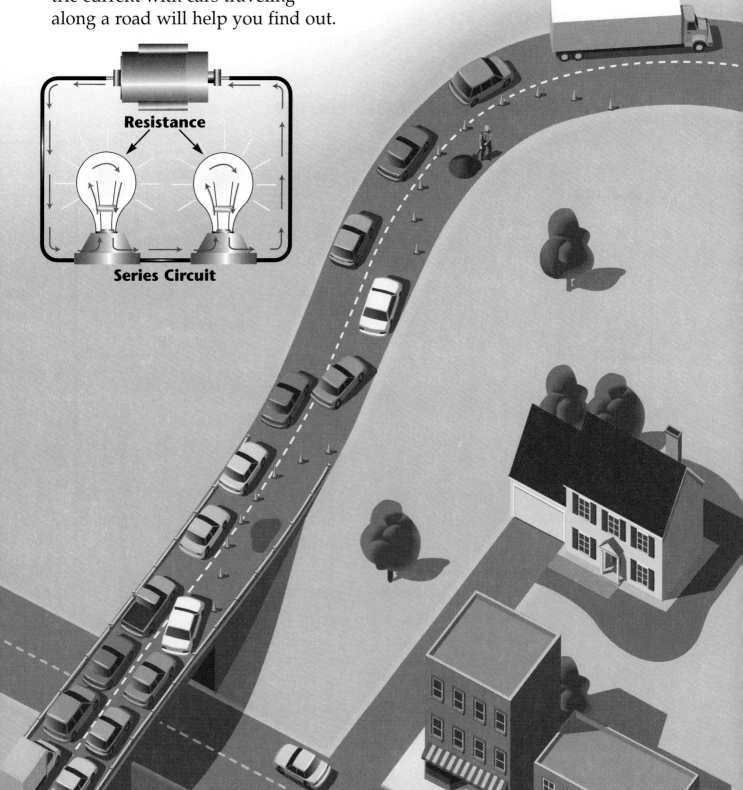

Resistance

Series Circuit

In a series circuit with two bulbs, current has only one path to follow. This path has one resistor after another in it. However, there are two paths along which current can flow in a parallel circuit. This diagram compares a parallel circuit with a split road. Each section of road has only one "resistor." More cars can travel along this road, just as more current can flow through a parallel circuit.

As you can see, more cars are traveling along this road than along the road with two narrow areas in a row. More paths are provided for cars to travel. Each path has only one narrow area, or "resistor."

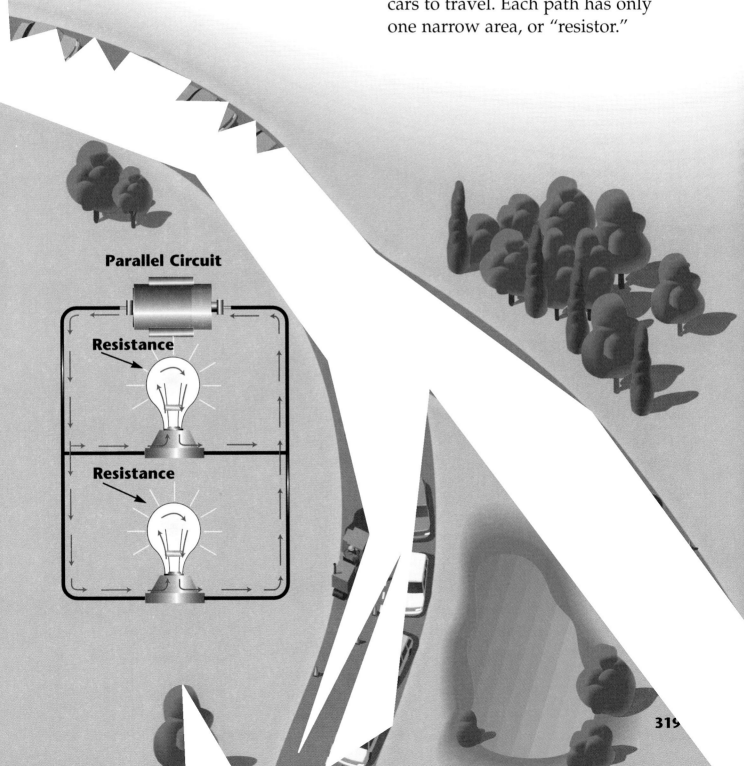

Parallel Circuit

Resistance

Resistance

SKILL BUILDER

Skill: Predicting

PREDICT IF IT WILL LIGHT

Making predictions is like telling the future. You can't be sure of the future. However, you can sometimes use what you know to make a good prediction.

How do you make good predictions? Look closely at each circuit. How is it similar to circuits you have seen before? How is it different? Use the information in the diagrams to predict what will happen in each circuit.

PROCEDURES

1. OBSERVE Study each circuit diagram carefully. Think about how current would flow in each circuit.

2. PREDICT In which circuits do you think the bulb or bulbs would light up? Record your predictions in your *Science Journal*.

3. PREDICT Compare circuits 4 and 5. Predict in which circuit the bulbs would be brightest.

CONCLUDE AND APPLY

1. IDENTIFY Which circuits are series circuits? Which are parallel circuits? Can you find a short circuit?

2. EXPLAIN How would you change the circuits that will not light? Make a model or draw a diagram to show how you would change them.

3. PREDICT Draw yet another circuit. Challenge a classmate to predict if the bulb or bulbs would light. Ask your classmate to explain his or her thoughts about the prediction.

MATERIALS

• *Science Journal*

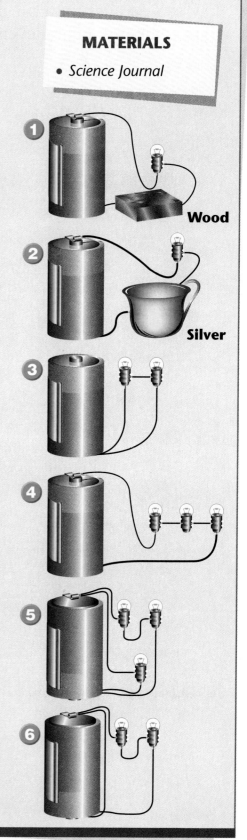

Wood

Silver

What Types of Circuits Are Found in Homes and Other Places?

Now that you know more about circuits, do you think those in homes and other places are series or parallel circuits? Why?

Electrical devices in homes and other places are connected in parallel circuits. If they were series circuits all the lights would go out if one bulb burnt out. Do you remember that the bulbs in the series circuit were dim? If many lights in your home were part of a series circuit, they would probably be so dim you couldn't see by them!

Circuits in homes and other places are controlled by switches. For example, flipping a light switch to the up position closes a circuit. The light goes on. Flipping the light switch on the wall down opens the circuit. The light goes off.

CLOSED CIRCUIT

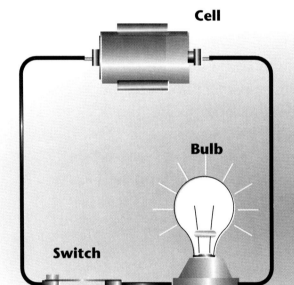

OPEN CIRCUIT

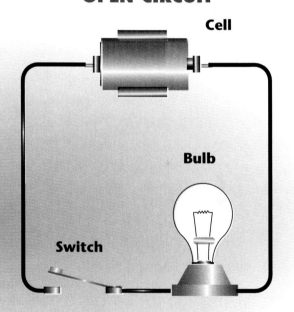

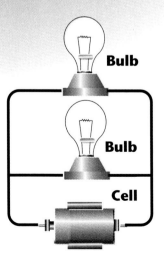

Brain Power

How can switches and one power source control more than one light in a parallel circuit? Where would you put switches to control each light in this circuit?

321

How Can Circuits in Homes Be Protected?

In the Skill Builder activity, circuit 6 would create a short circuit. That would happen because there is no resistance, such as a light bulb, in one of the paths. A short circuit is dangerous. Too much current flows in a short circuit. This can cause wires to heat up. Hot wires can start a fire. Too much current can also damage electrical devices.

One device that keeps too much electrical current from flowing through wires is called a **fuse** (fūz). A fuse has a thin strip of metal in it. The strip is a resistor, like the filament in a light bulb. When current flows through the resistor, it heats up. If a dangerously high current flows through it, the metal strip heats up only to a certain temperature. Then it melts. This creates an open circuit. The current stops flowing. Once a fuse melts, it cannot be reused. It must be replaced with a new fuse.

Most new homes do not have fuses. They are built with **circuit breakers** (sûr′kit brā′kərz). A circuit breaker is a switch that protects circuits. When a dangerously high current flows through the switch, the metal becomes heated. The overheated metal in the switch expands. This pushes the switch open. A spring holds the switch open creating an open circuit.

If some electrical devices stop working, an adult should check the circuit breakers. One or more of the switches will be in the *off* position if there was a short circuit. The switch needs to be pushed back to the *on* position. This should be done only once the problem is fixed, or another short circuit will occur.

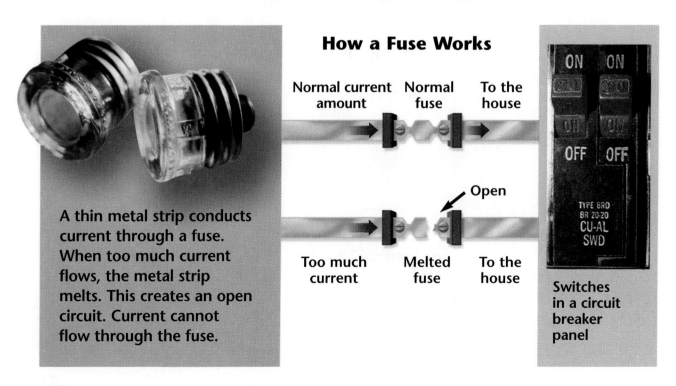

How a Fuse Works

A thin metal strip conducts current through a fuse. When too much current flows, the metal strip melts. This creates an open circuit. Current cannot flow through the fuse.

Normal current amount Normal fuse To the house

Too much current Melted fuse To the house Open

Switches in a circuit breaker panel

ON ON OFF OFF

TYPE BRD
BR 20-20
CU-AL
SWD

Understanding parallel and series circuits gives you a good idea of how the circuits in your home and school work. When you know how electricity travels through different types of circuits, you can control where it goes and what it does. You are also aware of safety issues. Imagine a world without different kinds of circuits. You couldn't control the individual lights or appliances in your home. Your life would be very different!

What would happen if the circuits in this room were series circuits?

REVIEW

1. What are two ways that a circuit can be connected using two light bulbs and one cell?

2. Describe the differences between a series and a parallel circuit in terms of how the parts are arranged.

3. Why do homes and other places have parallel circuits?

4. **PREDICT** Suppose you added an extra light bulb in a series circuit that already had two bulbs in it. Would the bulbs shine brighter or dimmer? Why?

5. **CRITICAL THINKING** *Apply* Should a fuse be in a series or a parallel circuit with the main power coming into a house? Explain.

WHY IT MATTERS THINK ABOUT IT
How would your life be different if only one type of circuit existed?

WHY IT MATTERS WRITE ABOUT IT
Write about a day when all the circuits in your home or school suddenly changed to series circuits.

Critical Circuits

Any electrical tool must have a complete circuit or current can't flow to make the tool work! Most circuits, like those in flashlights and video games, can fit into the palm of your hand.

Other circuits are gigantic! Electric power plants are linked in a giant circuit called a grid. Power demands from one plant can interrupt the whole circuit. On November 9, 1965,

one switch failed near Toronto, Canada. The power overload spread throughout eastern North America, causing a blackout over the entire region for hours!

Other circuits are tiny. The heart of a computer is a small silicon chip. It's about the size of

Greatly enlarged picture of a chip

a fingernail but may contain hundreds of thousands of tiny regions. Together they do the computer's "thinking." Each region must be connected to the others by a tiny circuit that's on the chip.

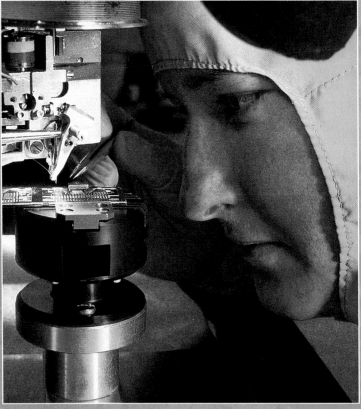

There can be hundreds of circuits on a single computer chip. That's why the computer-chip circuits are so tiny. If they were made of regular electrical parts with wires and switches, they'd cover a gym floor!

It's important to fit as many circuits as possible on a computer chip. Why? The farther apart they are, the farther the electrical signal has to travel and the slower the computer! The more circuits, the faster and more powerful the computer.

Creating the tiny circuits on computer chips is a difficult process. Workers wear protective suits to prevent dust and dirt from getting into the circuits.

DISCUSSION STARTER

1. What's the advantage of making smaller and smaller circuits for computer chips?

2. How small or large do you think circuits can get? Why?

To learn more about circuits, visit *www.mhschool.com/science* and enter the keyword MAZE.

*inter*NET
CONNECTION

SCIENCE WORDS

circuit p. 304

circuit
  breaker p. 322

closed
  circuit p. 305

conductor p. 295

current
  electricity p. 304

discharge p. 295

fuse p. 322

insulator p. 295

open circuit p. 305

parallel
  circuit p. 317

resistor p. 307

series circuit p .316

short circuit p. 308

static
  electricity p. 294

switch p. 309

USING SCIENCE WORDS

Number a paper from 1 to 10. Fill in 1 to 5 with words from the list above.

1. A buildup of electric charge that causes lightning is called ___?___.

2. A light bulb is a type of ___?___.

3. Current must flow through one device to get to another in a(n) ___?___.

4. A circuit that has a gap is a(n) ___?___.

5. A thin piece of metal in a(n) ___?___ melts when current is dangerously high.

6–10. Pick five words from the list above that were not used in 1 to 5, and use each in a sentence.

UNDERSTANDING SCIENCE IDEAS

11. How does a dry cell work to produce current?

12. What is the difference between a series and a parallel circuit?

USING IDEAS AND SKILLS

13. **READING SKILL: READING A DIAGRAM FOR INFORMATION** Look at the diagram on page 296. Describe the difference in charge between the ground and the bottom of the cloud.

14. **PREDICT** A company makes a lightning rod out of plastic. It is lighter, stronger, and cheaper to make than a metal lightning rod. Predict if this rod will work. Why or why not?

15. **THINKING LIKE A SCIENTIST** A fixture has six light bulbs in a row. How can you find out if the bulbs are wired in a series or a parallel circuit?

PROBLEMS and PUZZLES

Circuit Map How would you light a house? Draw a floor plan of a room or floor. Show where you would put lights. Map the circuits. Where will the electricity come from?

CHAPTER 10
MAKING AND USING
ELECTRICITY

Have you ever thought about where electricity comes from? In Chapter 9 you learned how a dry cell creates current. However, this current is not enough to power homes, businesses, and large machines. Most people know that power comes from a power station. Yet few think about how it is produced. In this chapter you will learn about ways people make and use electricity.

In this chapter you will have several opportunities to read for cause and effect. Knowing why something happens helps you to understand how events are connected.

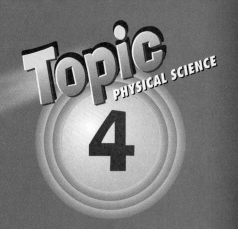
Electricity and Magnets

Did you know that a compass needle always points north? That is how a compass helps you find your way in unfamiliar places.

When Jenna's toy crane lifted a bar magnet, the magnet always pointed in the same direction. When the crane lifted a nonmagnet, it pointed in any direction. Jenna wondered if a hanging magnet is like a compass. Do you think so?

WHY IT MATTERS

Television and stereo speakers couldn't work without magnets.

SCIENCE WORDS

pole one of two ends of a magnet; where a magnet's pull is strongest

magnetic field a region of magnetic force around a magnet

electromagnet a temporary magnet created when current flows through wire wrapped in coils around an iron bar

EXPLORE

HYPOTHESIZE How does a bar magnet compare with a compass? Write a hypothesis in your *Science Journal.* How could you find out?

EXPLORE ACTIVITY

Investigate How a Bar Magnet Is Like a Compass

Play around with magnets to test how they compare with a compass.

MATERIALS

- 2 bar magnets
- 1 m of string
- compass
- ruler
- tape
- heavy book
- *Science Journal*

PROCEDURES

1. **OBSERVE** How do the bar magnets interact when you place them next to each other in different positions?

2. **PREDICT** Which way will the bar magnet point if you hang it as shown? Record your prediction in your *Science Journal.*

3. **OBSERVE** Test your prediction. Record the results.

4. **COMPARE** Place the compass on a flat surface away from the magnets. Compare the directions in which the compass and magnet point.

5. **OBSERVE** Hold the compass near the hanging magnet. What happens?

CONCLUDE AND APPLY

1. **COMMUNICATE** How do the two magnets interact with each other?

2. **COMPARE** How did your hanging magnet compare with other students' magnets?

3. **COMMUNICATE** What happened when you brought the compass near the hanging magnet?

4. **INFER** Of what must a compass be made?

GOING FURTHER: Problem Solving

5. **INFER** What do you think was pulling the magnet and compass?

How Are a Compass and a Magnet Alike?

The Explore Activity showed that Jenna was correct. The hanging magnet pointed north, just as the compass did. Magnets also interacted when they were placed next to each other. Study these pages to learn more about the properties of magnets and compasses.

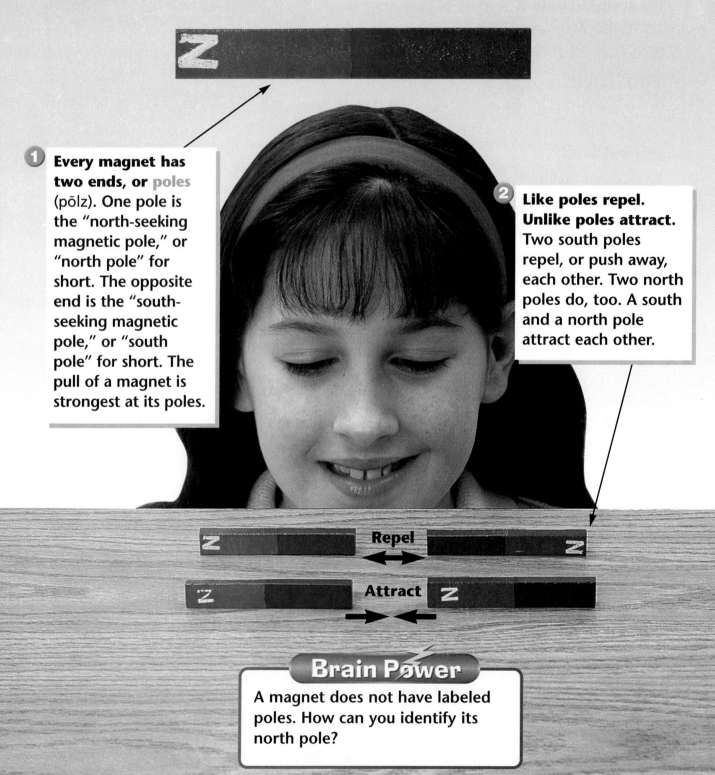

1 Every magnet has two ends, or poles (pōlz). One pole is the "north-seeking magnetic pole," or "north pole" for short. The opposite end is the "south-seeking magnetic pole," or "south pole" for short. The pull of a magnet is strongest at its poles.

2 Like poles repel. Unlike poles attract. Two south poles repel, or push away, each other. Two north poles do, too. A south and a north pole attract each other.

Repel

Attract

Brain Power
A magnet does not have labeled poles. How can you identify its north pole?

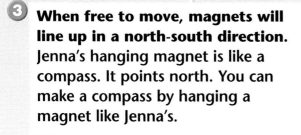

3 **When free to move, magnets will line up in a north-south direction.** Jenna's hanging magnet is like a compass. It points north. You can make a compass by hanging a magnet like Jenna's.

North

4 **A compass is a magnet.** The needle of a compass is a small magnet. It is attached to the base by a small pin. The pin does not move but allows the needle to turn toward Earth's North Pole.

331

How Magnets Interact

HYPOTHESIZE It seems that there is an invisible force at work between magnets. What do you think causes magnets to interact the way they do? Write a hypothesis in your *Science Journal.*

MATERIALS

- safety goggles
- 2 bar magnets
- piece of white paper
- iron filings in a sealed plastic bag
- tape
- *Science Journal*

PROCEDURES

 Safety: Wear safety goggles.

1. **OBSERVE** Tape a bar magnet flat on your desk. Place the paper over it. Put the bag of iron filings over the paper. Sketch the pattern of the filings in your *Science Journal.*

2. **OBSERVE** Repeat step 1 using two bar magnets with their poles 2 cm apart. Try different north/south combinations. Sketch each setup and the patterns you see.

CONCLUDE AND APPLY

1. **OBSERVE** Describe the pattern of the filings when like and unlike poles were next to each other.

2. **COMPARE** How was the pattern of a single bar magnet different from the pattern of two magnets?

Why Do a Hanging Magnet and Compass Turn?

What attracted Jenna's hanging magnet and made it line up in a north-south direction? The answer may surprise you. Earth itself is a magnet.

Imagine a huge bar magnet running along Earth's center. This magnet would create a region of magnetic force called a **magnetic field** (mag net′ik fēld). Jenna's magnet lined up with Earth's magnetic field in a north-south direction. In other words the north-seeking magnetic pole faced Earth's north magnetic pole. The south-seeking magnetic pole faced Earth's south magnetic pole. You can't see a magnetic field. However, the iron filings in the Quick Lab let you "see" the magnetic field of bar magnets.

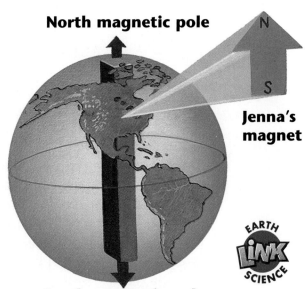

North magnetic pole

Jenna's magnet

South magnetic pole

EARTH
LINK
SCIENCE

Jenna's magnet lined up with Earth's magnetic field.

Where Do Magnets Come From?

A magnet is a material or device that attracts items containing the elements iron, nickel, or cobalt (kō'bôlt).

About 2,000 years ago, people from an area called Magnesia (mag nē'shə) found rocks that would attract small pieces of iron. The rocks are called magnetite (mag'ni tīt´). They contain magnetized iron.

What gives a magnet its properties? A piece of magnetized iron, like all matter, is made up of particles. Each particle of iron has its own magnetic field. When the particles are all lined up in the same direction, their magnetic fields act together. This makes the piece of iron have a strong magnetic field.

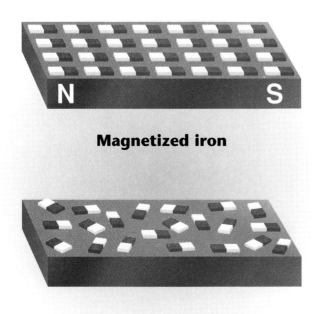

Magnetized iron

Nonmagnetized iron

Magnets can also be created using electric current. Current running in a wire creates a weak magnetic field. When current flows a magnetic field forms around the wire. When the current is turned off, the magnetic field goes away.

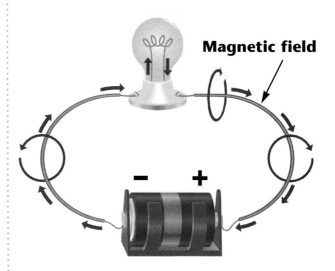

Magnetic field

You can make a stronger magnetic field by winding the wire in loops around an iron bar. When current flows this creates a temporary magnet called an **electromagnet** (i lek´trō mag'nit).

Electromagnet

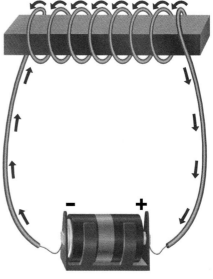

333

QUICK LAB
MATH LINK

Stronger Electromagnets

HYPOTHESIZE What will make an electromagnet stronger? Write a hypothesis in your *Science Journal.*

MATERIALS

- nail
- 2 D-cells and holders
- wire with stripped ends
- 10 paper clips
- *Science Journal*

PROCEDURES

1. Wind the wire 20 times around the nail near its head. Attach each end of the wire to the D-cell to complete the circuit.

2. **OBSERVE** Record in your *Science Journal* how many paper clips your electromagnet can hold.

3. **EXPERIMENT** Repeat using two D-cells in series. Record how many paper clips the nail held.

4. **EXPERIMENT** Wind the wire 20 more times. Repeat steps 2 and 3.

CONCLUDE AND APPLY

INTERPRET DATA How did increasing current affect the strength of the electromagnet? Increasing the number of coils?

How Are Electromagnets Used?

This junkyard crane uses a powerful electromagnet. It attracts all items made of iron, steel, nickel, and cobalt.

Electromagnets also have many other uses. Doctors use electromagnets to take iron splinters out of a patient's skin. Recyclers use them to separate scrap metals. Electromagnets are also used in machines such as tape players, bells, motors, buzzers, loudspeakers, and televisions.

A junkyard crane uses an electromagnet to move large pieces of metal.

How Does a Doorbell Work?

An electric doorbell is made up of an electromagnet and a power source. Figure A shows the doorbell circuit before you push the button. The gap leaves the circuit open. No current flows.

Figure B shows that when you push the button, the gap closes. Current flows. This pulls the electromagnet and makes the hammer hit the bell.

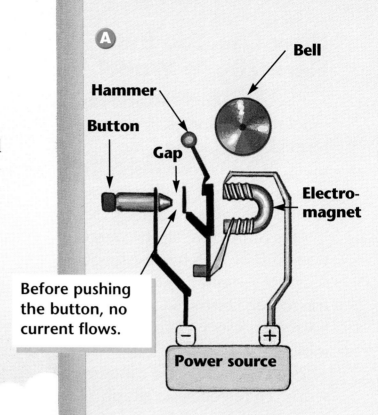

A

Bell

Hammer

Button

Gap

Electro-magnet

Before pushing the button, no current flows.

− +

Power source

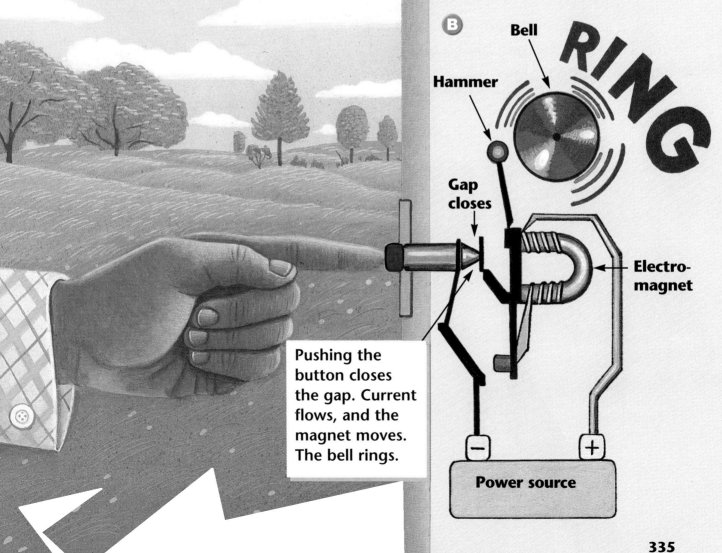

B

Bell

RING

Hammer

Gap closes

Electro-magnet

Pushing the button closes the gap. Current flows, and the magnet moves. The bell rings.

− +

Power source

335

How Can You Put Electricity to Work?

Electric motors are clean and quiet power sources. They transform electrical energy into movement, or mechanical energy. This energy can power video recorders, some appliances, and other devices.

One of the first electric motors was built in 1829 by an American scientist, Joseph Henry. In his electric motor, electromagnets made a beam that was balanced on a pivot move up and down.

How does an electric motor work? Here you see a simple electric motor made of D-cells, paper clips, a coil of wire, and a bar magnet. The Explore and Quick Lab activities showed how magnetic fields can interact with each other.

You also learned that current passing through a conductor creates a magnetic field.

When the switch of an electric motor is closed, current passes through the coiled wire. This creates an electromagnet. When the bar magnet is brought near it, their magnetic fields interact. As the two magnets attract and repel each other, they make the coil spin.

**Joseph Henry
(1797–1878)**

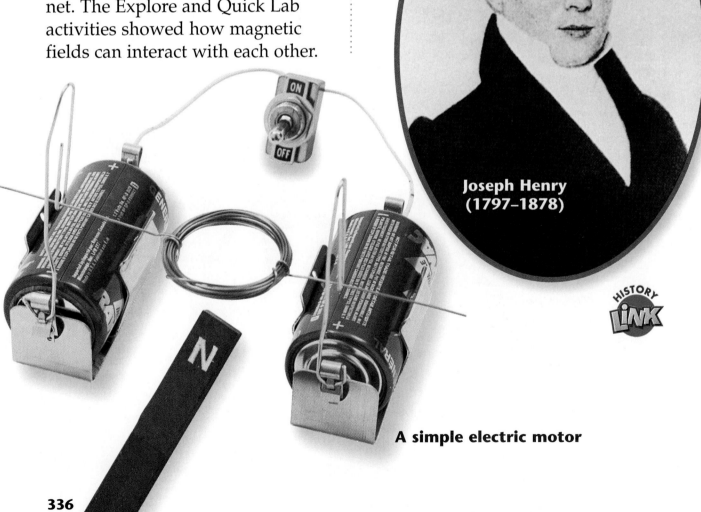

A simple electric motor

WHY IT MATTERS

The use of magnets has come a long way. By A.D. 1000 Chinese travelers used magnetic stones to find their way. In 1820 Danish scientist Hans Oersted discovered that magnetism and electricity were linked. By the 1880s electric motors were powering many different kinds of machines.

Today electromagnets play important roles in our everyday lives. They are used to separate recycled materials, to sound car horns, and to record data on computer disks. Cassette players, stereo speakers, and televisions contain electromagnets. Electromagnets are useful because we can change parts of the system to turn them on and off, and make them as strong as needed.

REVIEW

1. How are a magnet and a compass similar?

2. What happens when like poles of magnets are brought together? When opposite poles are brought together?

3. What is an electric motor? What does it do?

4. **COMPARE** How is a magnetic stone different from an electromagnet?

5. **CRITICAL THINKING** *Analyze* Would a compass be useful on a spaceship in outer space? Why or why not?

WHY IT MATTERS THINK ABOUT IT
Why isn't it a good idea to store computer disks near a television, VCR, or stereo speaker? Think about what a warning on a package of disks should say.

WHY IT MATTERS WRITE ABOUT IT
Based on everything you've learned and observed, in your own words, write a definition of an electromagnet.

READING SKILL Write a short paragraph that explains what causes a doorbell to ring.

Flips, Slides,

Let's create geometric patterns by moving figures around. Try these three ways.

Flip It!

Flip a figure over a line, and the second figure looks like a mirror image of the first! Hold out your hands in front of you, palms up. Spread out your fingers. The shape of your right hand is like a mirror image of your left. Check it out. Flip your left hand over onto your right, palms facing each other. Then open your hands!

Slide It!

Slide a figure across a line. The second figure looks the same, but it's in a different place!

Turn It!

Turn a figure around a point on a line. Imagine holding one end of the figure and moving the other end in a circle!

and Turns

One of those patterns is made inside an electric motor! There's a metal coil sitting between the poles of a magnet. Electric current flows through the coil and magnetizes it. Because it's between the magnet's poles, the coil spins as its magnetic field interacts with the magnet's magnetic field. That movement keeps the motor running. The spin follows one of the geometric patterns. Which one do you think it is?

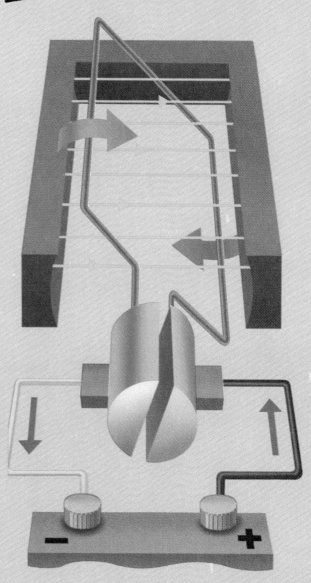

DISCUSSION STARTER

1. Why does the coil in an electric motor spin?

2. Which of the geometric patterns do you think a coil in an electric motor represents? Why?

To learn more about geometric patterns, visit *www.mhschool.com/science* and enter the keyword FLIPS.

*inter*NET
CONNECTION

WHY IT MATTERS

Electricity may have to travel a long way from where it is made to where it is used.

Making Electricity

Have you ever been in a blackout? A blackout occurs when the electrical system in an area stops working. What happened during the blackout? How long did it last?

In 1965 a blackout affected the eastern United States. Cities from Boston to New York had no power! You may not think much about the electricity in your home or where it comes from—until it's gone!

SCIENCE WORDS

direct current current that flows in one direction through a circuit

alternating current current that flows in a circuit first in one direction, then in the opposite direction

generator a device that creates alternating current

volt a unit for measuring the force that makes negative charges flow

transformer a device in which alternating current in one coil produces current in a second coil

EXPLORE

HYPOTHESIZE You know that electric current can produce a magnetic field. Do you think that a magnetic field can produce electric current? Write a hypothesis in your *Science Journal.* How can you test your ideas?

Investigate Another Way to Make Electric Current

Test another way to make electric current using wires and a magnet.

MATERIALS

- "current detector"
- paper-towel tube wrapped with enameled wire
- bar magnet
- D-cell
- D-cell holder
- tape
- *Science Journal*

PROCEDURES

1. Turn your "current detector" until the needle points north. Line up the wire loops with the needle. Tape the detector to your desk.

2. OBSERVE Connect one end of the wire to the D-cell in its holder. Briefly touch the other end of the wire to the other end of the cell. Record your observations in your *Science Journal*.

3. Obtain a cardboard tube wrapped in wire from your teacher. Connect the current detector to the ends of the wires to make a circuit.

4. OBSERVE Insert the bar magnet into the tube. Observe what happens to the detector.

5. PREDICT What will happen if you take out the magnet? Try it. Record your observations.

CONCLUDE AND APPLY

1. OBSERVE What happened to the current detector when current passed through the wire?

2. INTERPRET DATA What did the loops of wire around the compass form when current passed through them?

3. INFER How does the moving compass needle show that current passed through the wire?

GOING FURTHER: Problem Solving

4. INFER What made a current in the wire?

What Is Another Way to Make Electric Current?

In Topic 4 you learned that electric current creates a magnetic field. The Explore Activity showed that the reverse is also true. A magnet can create electric current.

Here are three ways to make electric current.

1 Move a magnet inside a closed loop or coil.

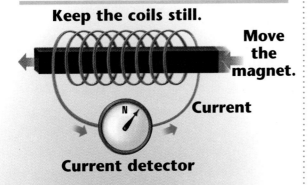

Keep the coils still.

Move the magnet.

Current

Current detector

2 Keep the magnet steady, and move the coil.

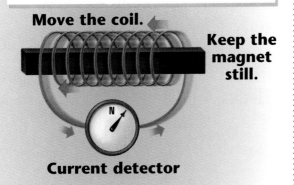

Move the coil.

Keep the magnet still.

Current detector

3 Change chemical energy to electric energy using a cell.

Current flow

Different Types of Current

There are two types of current. The type of current that you have studied was created by dry cells. It is called **direct current** (di rekt' kûr'ənt). Direct current is like a one-way street. It flows in one direction through the circuit. Cells and batteries make direct current.

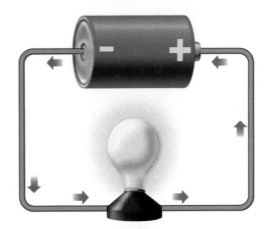

Negative charges flow from the negative terminal along the wire, through the light bulb, and on to the positive terminal. It flows in only one direction.

In the Explore Activity, the compass needle moved in one direction when the magnet was placed into the tube. When the magnet was pulled out, the needle moved the other way. This is like the current that flows in your home.

The two-way current in your home is called **alternating current** (ôl'tər nāt'ing kûr'ənt), or AC for short. The current first flows in one direction. Then it flows in the opposite direction. This happens many times every second. It is so quick that lights don't flicker.

What Makes the Electricity You Use?

Where do you think alternating current comes from? A device that creates alternating current is called a **generator** (jen′ə rā′tər). How does a generator work? These diagrams will show you.

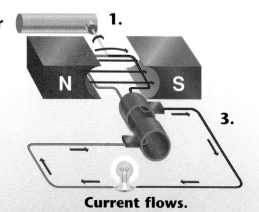

Outside power

1.

3.

Current flows.

① A generator works by spinning a coil between the poles of a powerful magnet.

③ Current flows as the red side of the coil passes up through the magnetic field.

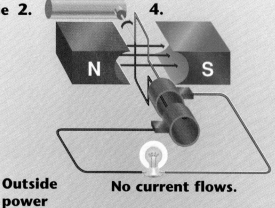

Outside power 2.

4.

No current flows.

Outside power

② An outside force spins the coil. The force may come from a gasoline engine, from steam heated by a coal or nuclear power plant, or from running water.

④ In this position no part of the coil passes through the magnetic field. No current flows.

5.

Current flows in opposite direction.

⑤ Now the red side of the coil passes down through the field instead of up. Current flows in the opposite direction. The cycle continues as the coil spins. The current changes direction many times every second.

READING 𝒩 DIAGRAMS

1. **REPRESENT** Make a list showing some things that power a generator.
2. **DISCUSS** How is a generator different from what was built in the Explore Activity?

Are There Other Types of Cells?

A cell uses the energy stored in chemicals to make electric current. In Topic 2 you learned about dry cells. A dry cell has a chemical acid paste around a carbon rod. Another type of cell is a *wet cell*.

In the simplest case, a wet cell contains two different metal bars placed in a liquid. The liquid contains certain chemicals and is an acid. A car battery is made up of many connected wet cells.

The negative and positive terminals of a cell are called *electrodes* (i lek'trōdz). The positive electrode in some wet cells is made of copper. The acid strips away negative charges from the copper. This leaves the copper bar positive.

The negative electrode is made of the metal zinc. The negative charges that leave the copper move to the zinc bar. This makes it have a negative charge.

When you attach a wire between the electrodes, current from a wet cell flows one way only. It is direct current.

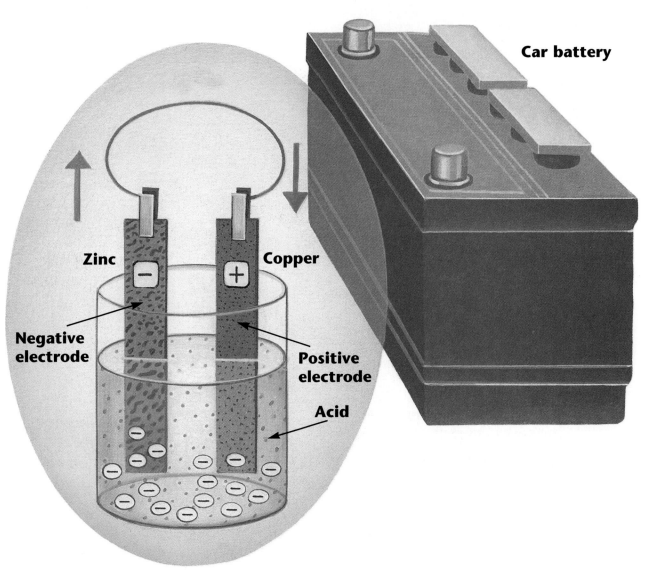

Car battery

Zinc

Copper

Negative electrode

Positive electrode

Acid

Can the Power of a Cell Be Measured?

Have you ever used batteries? If so, what did you use them for? Did you notice that they come in many different sizes? Each battery is labeled to show how many **volts** (vōlts) it has. A volt is the unit used to measure the force that makes negative charges flow. This force is called *voltage* (vōl'tij). A battery is a series of cells that are connected to produce extra voltage.

How much is a volt? A flashlight battery puts out 1.5 volts. Can it give you a shock? Not likely. A car battery puts out 12 volts. It can give you a shock. Your wall socket typically puts out 110 volts. This is enough to kill a person. Never touch any part of a circuit that is plugged into the wall. It is dangerous!

How many volts does this battery put out?

Build a Wet Cell

HYPOTHESIZE How do you think you can make a wet cell? Write a hypothesis in your *Science Journal*.

MATERIALS
- safety goggles
- $\frac{1}{2}$ c of distilled vinegar
- plastic cup
- current detector from the Explore Activity
- copper strip
- zinc strip
- tape
- *Science Journal*

PROCEDURES

 Safety: Wear safety goggles.

1. Put on your goggles. Pour the vinegar into the cup.

2. **OBSERVE** Tape one metal strip to each end of the current detector. Place the metal strips in the vinegar. Record your observations of the detector in your *Science Journal*.

CONCLUDE AND APPLY

1. **OBSERVE** Did your wet cell produce current? How do you know?

2. **COMMUNICATE** What function did the vinegar have in your experiment?

What Happens to Current Before It Reaches Your Home?

Power stations near your home have powerful electric generators. Huge magnets inside these generators spin inside huge coils. This produces current. The energy to spin the huge magnets comes from water, wind, or some kind of fuel.

A typical power plant puts out 25,000 volts or more of electrical force. This is far too much to use in your house. The voltage is lowered by use of a **transformer** (trans fôr′mər). A transformer is made up of two wire coils. Alternating current travels through the first coil. This produces a current in the second coil.

Voltage generated by this power plant is reduced by transformers.

In transformer A the right side has twice as many coils as the left. This means that current going from left to right doubles in voltage.

In transformer B the left side has twice as many coils. The voltage of current going from left to right is cut in half.

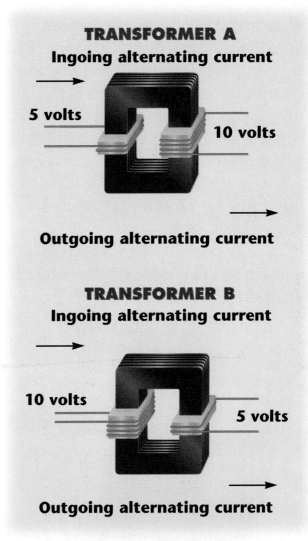

TRANSFORMER A
Ingoing alternating current

5 volts

10 volts

Outgoing alternating current

TRANSFORMER B
Ingoing alternating current

10 volts

5 volts

Outgoing alternating current

Brain Power

How many loops would you put in each side of a transformer to change voltage in a battery from 60 volts to 180 volts? Draw a picture of the transformer.

346

SKILL BUILDER

MATH LINK

Skill: Using Numbers

TRANSFORMERS AND NUMBERS

Numbers help you understand how things work in the real world. In this activity you will be looking for a pattern in the volts going into and out of five different transformers.

MATERIALS

- calculator (optional)
- *Science Journal*

PROCEDURES

1. The left side of transformer A has 10 times as many loops as the right side. Ten times as many volts go into the transformer as go out. The 110 volts going in are reduced 10 times to 11 volts.

2. The right side of transformer B has 10 times as many loops as the left side. Ten times fewer volts go into the transformer as go out. The 15 volts going in are increased 10 times to 150 volts.

3. **INTERPRET DATA** Do you notice a pattern? Write the number of volts for diagrams C–E in your *Science Journal*.

CONCLUDE AND APPLY

1. **INTERPRET DATA** What is the pattern that you noticed in the transformers?

2. **COMPARE** In which transformers is the voltage increased? Decreased? Make a table of your results.

A
Ingoing current
11 volts
110 volts
Outgoing current

B
Ingoing current
150 volts
15 volts
Outgoing current

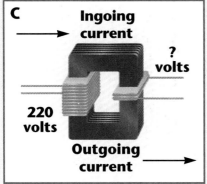

C
Ingoing current
? volts
220 volts
Outgoing current

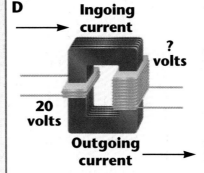

D
Ingoing current
? volts
20 volts
Outgoing current

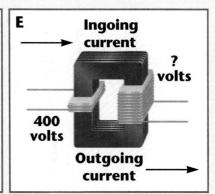

E
Ingoing current
? volts
400 volts
Outgoing current

How Does Current Get to Your Home?

Do you think there are large magnets inside your home producing alternating current? Probably not! How do you think current gets to your home? This diagram shows how current gets from a power plant to your home.

1 A power plant gets energy from wind, water, fossil fuel, or nuclear power.

3 Current with high voltage is dangerous. It travels on wires often placed high above the ground.

2 A transformer increases the voltage. High-voltage current is best for traveling long distances. It loses less energy along the way.

4 Another transformer decreases the voltage.

An even smaller transformer decreases the voltage.

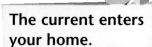

The current enters your home.

READING N

1. **DISCUSS** Why is high voltage used to travel long distances?
2. **WRITE** List the steps showing what happens to current as it travels from a power plant to your home.

Knowing how to make and use electricity safely is important. We depend on electricity every day to help us perform a variety of tasks. Giant generators produce current that travels all across the continent. Transformers allow us to change voltage to meet our needs. It also makes electricity safer to use.

The electricity we use every day is provided by a generator that works on the ideas and discoveries of scientists like Michael Faraday, Joseph Henry, and many others. Each deserves a big "Thank you!"

HISTORY LINK

Michael Faraday demonstrated the ideas used to make electric motors.

REVIEW

1. What are some ways, other than a dry cell, to make electricity?

2. Use a model to explain how a generator produces alternating current.

3. How are a wet cell and a dry cell similar? Different?

4. **USE NUMBERS** Alternating current going into a transformer has 200 volts. The current coming out has 20 volts. How many loops of wire might each coil have?

5. **CRITICAL THINKING** *Analyze* What do you think might happen if a transformer along the way from a power station was not working properly?

WHY IT MATTERS **THINK ABOUT IT**
Design a circuit to light a room or to light a matching-game board. Share your design with a classmate.

WHY IT MATTERS **WRITE ABOUT IT**
Three hundred years ago, no one dreamed of electric lights. Early experiments with electricity were often very dangerous. What uses do you think electricity might have 300 years from now? Do you think it will be even safer to use?

Current Jobs

Do you like to take things apart? Can you put them back together again? Maybe you'd be interested in becoming an electrician!

"What do electricians do?" you might ask. Some put wiring and other electrical parts in new buildings. Others repair electrical parts in older buildings. Some just fix problems.

Electricians must know about all kinds of electrical parts. They must be able to find and fix electrical problems. They also must know how to handle and care for tools.

Electricians must make safe connections and not overload electrical systems. Electricians must check their work for safety, too. Loose or broken wires can cause fires or shock people.

To become an electrician, most people help other electricians for a few years. They also take at least 144 hours of classes each year. In most cities electricians must be licensed. People must pass a test to get the license.

Appliance repairers fix washers, TVs, toasters, and other electrical machines.

They spend at least six months learning on the job. Some take one- or two-year training programs. They also have to pass a test, if they plan to fix refrigerators or air conditioners. Those contain harmful chemicals. Repairers must know how to keep the chemicals out of the air.

Many new machines have electronic parts. They need fewer repairs. That means fewer jobs for repairers. Those who know how to fix electronic parts get the most jobs.

DISCUSSION STARTER

1. Why do electricians need to work carefully?

2. Which is more likely to need an appliance repairer, a new home or an older home? Why?

Would you like to be an electrician or an appliance repairer? Why or why not?

To learn more about electricians, visit **www.mhschool.com/science** and enter the keyword WIRING.

*inter*NET CONNECTION

Topic
PHYSICAL SCIENCE
6

WHY IT MATTERS

Electrical energy changes into many other forms of energy.

SCIENCE WORDS

energy transformation
a change of energy from one form to another

radiate to travel in all directions

Transforming Electricity

Can you help this group of friends? They have turned on several lights to help them see how all the model pieces fit together. Soon they begin to feel warm. "Boy, it's hot in here!" Maria says. "It certainly is," replies Marco. Why do you think it is so hot? "I bet it's all these lights we have on," Bruce says. What do you think?

EXPLORE

HYPOTHESIZE Can the light energy of even small flashlight bulbs be changed into heat? Write a hypothesis in your *Science Journal.* Test your ideas.

Design Your Own Experiment

CAN LIGHT ENERGY CHANGE?

PROCEDURES

1. Set up a circuit like this one. You can set up a different circuit if you like.

2. USE VARIABLES How would you test to see if painting a bulb affects how warm it gets? Do you think changing the outside of a plain bulb in another way might make it get warmer? Test your ideas. Record your results in your *Science Journal.*

3. USE VARIABLES Can you think of any other variable that might affect how warm a bulb gets? Test your ideas. Record your results.

MATERIALS

- flashlight bulb
- flashlight bulb painted black
- 2 bulb holders
- 5 pieces of hookup wire, 20 cm each
- 2 D-cells
- 2 D-cell holders
- small pieces of foil and cloth
- *Science Journal*

CONCLUDE AND APPLY

1. COMPARE Did you feel some heat energy in any of the bulbs? What variables were you testing? What materials were you using?

2. INFER What if some light bulbs felt warmer? How can you explain what might have caused that to happen?

3. INTERPRET DATA Do you think light energy can be transformed into heat energy? Why or why not?

GOING FURTHER: Problem Solving

4. EXPERIMENT What other variables might affect changing light energy into heat energy? How could you test your idea in an experiment?

Can Electrical Energy Be Changed?

In the Explore Activity, the painted light bulb felt warmer than the unpainted bulb. What do you think was going on? The answer is an example of an **energy transformation** (en′ər jē trans′fər mā′shən). An energy transformation is a change of energy from one form to another. How does this happen?

Light energy normally **radiates** (rā′dē āts′), or travels in all directions through space. The black paint blocked the light and absorbed its energy. The bulb got hotter and hotter as it absorbed more and more light energy.

Light energy that can't escape from the bulb as light is radiated by the black surface as heat.

In this topic you will learn about five different ways we use changed energy every day.

How Can Electrical Energy Be Changed?

Into heat energy

Into sound energy

Into mechanical energy, the energy of moving things

Into chemical energy

Into light energy

How Can Electrical Energy Be Changed into Heat Energy?

How many appliances in your home create heat? Make a list. Does your list include items like an iron, an electric stove, a toaster, and a hair dryer? All of these things need electricity to work.

How do you think the electrical energy is changed into heat energy? In Topic 2 you learned that a resistor is a material that does not conduct electricity well. In other words a resistor is a poor conductor. One of the most common places to find a resistor is in a typical light bulb. Some, not all, of the electrical energy going into the bulb produces light energy. What do you think happens to the rest?

Have you ever accidentally touched a lit light bulb? It probably felt warm, or even hot. That is because some electrical energy was changed into heat energy.

Many of the devices on your list contain wires that are good resistors. These wires are looped into coils. This allows a long wire to fit into a small space. The more coils an appliance has, the hotter it can get.

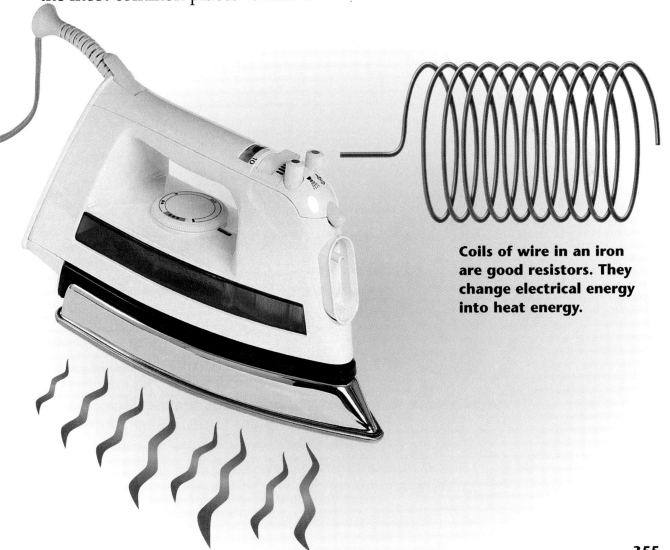

Coils of wire in an iron are good resistors. They change electrical energy into heat energy.

How Can Electrical Energy Be Changed into Sound Energy?

How do you think loudspeakers and earphones work? They change electrical energy into sound energy.

Loudspeakers are used in radios, telephones, CD players, and other devices that produce sound. Sound is created by vibration. The job of the speaker is to get a thin cone to vibrate. The cone's vibrations produce sounds.

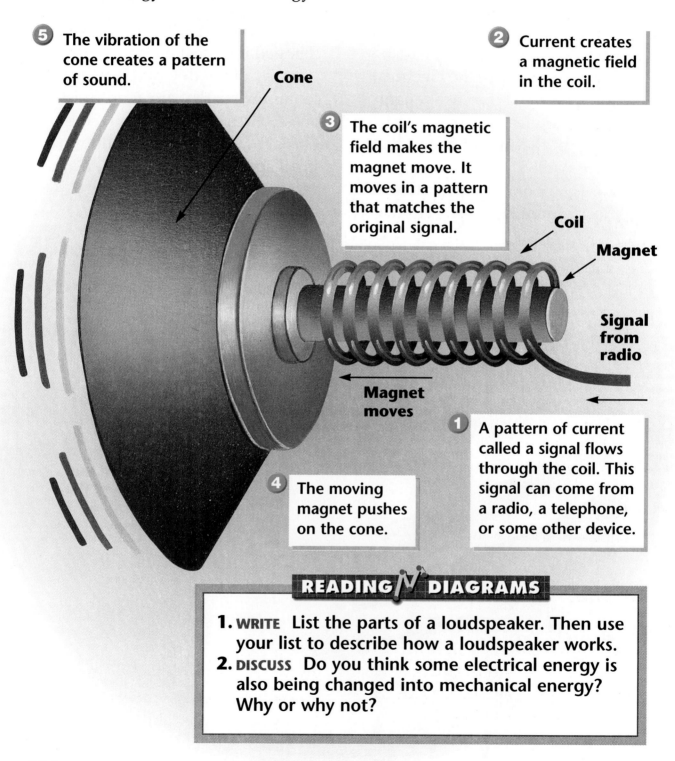

5 The vibration of the cone creates a pattern of sound.

Cone

2 Current creates a magnetic field in the coil.

3 The coil's magnetic field makes the magnet move. It moves in a pattern that matches the original signal.

Coil

Magnet

Signal from radio

Magnet moves

4 The moving magnet pushes on the cone.

1 A pattern of current called a signal flows through the coil. This signal can come from a radio, a telephone, or some other device.

READING ✐ DIAGRAMS

1. **WRITE** List the parts of a loudspeaker. Then use your list to describe how a loudspeaker works.
2. **DISCUSS** Do you think some electrical energy is also being changed into mechanical energy? Why or why not?

How Can Electrical Energy Be Changed into Chemical Energy?

Have you ever left a video game or flashlight on too long? What happened? After some time the batteries probably "died." The chemicals in the cells were used up. The chemical reaction stopped. The cells could no longer produce an electric current.

When this happens the batteries must be thrown out. However, don't just throw them in the kitchen trash. Remember, cells contain chemicals that can harm someone if the cell is broken open. Place the batteries in a sealed plastic bag. Give them to an adult. He or she should place them with other dangerous materials. Most communities have a recycling center for hazardous household wastes.

Have you ever seen a battery like this one? It is called a *rechargeable* (rē chär'jə bəl) *battery*. A battery made of rechargeable cells works like a normal battery, except that the chemical reactions in it can be reversed.

The batteries are placed into a device called a recharger. The recharger needs to be plugged into an electrical outlet. The recharger produces a current in the opposite direction. This causes the chemical reaction to be reversed. After a time the cells are recharged. Rechargeable batteries can be used again and again.

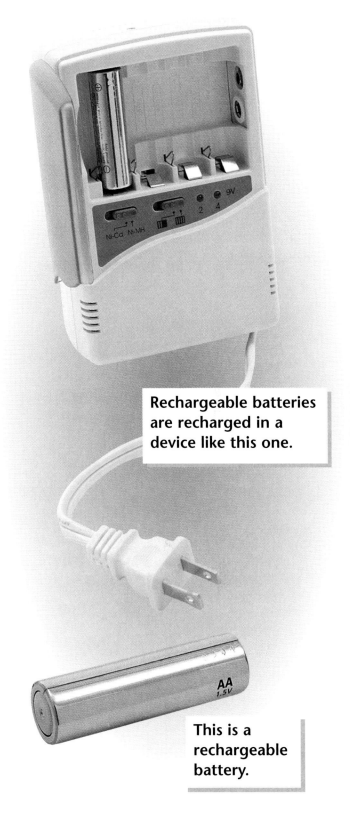

Rechargeable batteries are recharged in a device like this one.

This is a rechargeable battery.

Brain Power
How can using rechargeable batteries be good for the environment?

357

How Can Electrical Energy Be Changed into Mechanical Energy?

In Topic 4 you learned that an electric motor changes electrical energy into mechanical energy. How can you use the mechanical energy of a spinning motor to do something? One answer is gears (gîrz). Gears transfer motion and force from one source to another.

Here you see a simple drawing of a toy car. How can the electrical energy from the motor make the car's wheels spin? First, review the motor. A battery sends current through a coil. The coil then spins between the two poles of a magnet. The coil is connected to a gear. As the coil spins, the gear spins clockwise.

As this gear turns, it transfers its motion to another gear. The other gear is perpendicular to the first. It is also attached to the car's axle. As this gear turns, it turns the axle. The car moves forward.

Gears can be used to do other things than move the car forward. If the direction of the first gear is reversed, the car can go in reverse. The car can also be made to go faster. It could pull a load. These things can be done using different gear combinations or different-sized gears.

A SIMPLE MOTOR

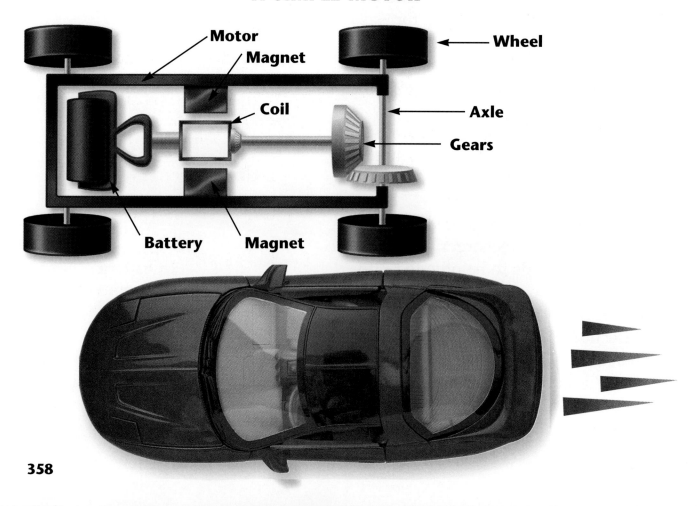

Motor
Magnet
Coil
Wheel
Axle
Gears
Battery
Magnet

How Can Electrical Energy Be Changed into Light Energy?

A television changes a pattern of electrical energy into a pattern of light energy and some sound energy.

How does a television work to make images? A signal, or pattern of current, comes from a cable or antenna. The signal is fed into the television's electron gun. The signal is translated into a beam of negatively charged particles. The electron gun shoots the beam at a screen.

The beam travels back and forth across the screen. It makes hundreds of lines. The screen is bright where many particles hit it. It is dim where few particles hit it. The gun makes an entirely new pattern of lines 60 times each second.

DIAGRAM OF TELEVISION

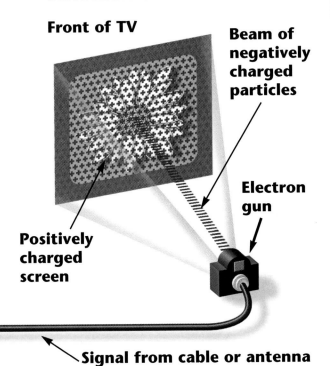

Front of TV

Beam of negatively charged particles

Electron gun

Positively charged screen

Signal from cable or antenna

QUICK LAB

Identifying Energy Transformations

HYPOTHESIZE What types of clues can you use to identify types of energy transformations in your classroom? Write a hypothesis in your *Science Journal.*

MATERIALS
- *Science Journal*

PROCEDURES

1. **OBSERVE** Look around the classroom. Which items use electrical energy? Make a list in your *Science Journal.*

2. **INFER** Which items change electrical energy into another form of energy? What type of energy? Record your observations in your *Science Journal.*

3. **CLASSIFY** Classify the items into groups based on how they change electrical energy.

CONCLUDE AND APPLY

1. **IDENTIFY** Into what types of energy did the items change electrical energy?

2. **EXPLAIN** What clues did you use to help you identify how the electrical energy was changed?

359

In this topic you learned about five different ways we use changed energy every day. Study these pictures carefully. What types of energy transformations are taking place in each one?

ELECTRICAL ENERGY

Electrical energy makes this coil on an electric stove glow red-hot.

Sound ENERGY

Heat ENERGY

Into what types of energy does a television transform electrical energy? What lets you see the lion on the screen? What lets you hear it roar?

These bulbs are called infrared (in′frə red′) light bulbs. Infrared bulbs are often used to keep prepared foods warm in restaurants. Why do you think they are called infrared? Into what other type of energy is the electrical energy being transformed?

Light ENERGY

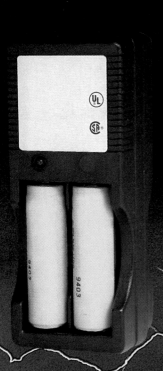

The chemical reactions within a rechargeable battery can be reversed. The recharger produces a current in the opposite direction. This causes the chemical reaction to be reversed. The batteries are recharged and can be used again.

Chemical ENERGY

Into what types of energy does this power tool transform electrical energy? Why is such a tool useful?

This toy gets its power from batteries. Into what types of energy do you think the electrical energy is transformed? Why do you think so?

Mechanical ENERGY

READING /\/ DIAGRAMS

1. **WRITE** Into what other types of energy can electrical energy be transformed? Make a list.
2. **DISCUSS** Did you use electrical energy that was transformed into another type of energy today? What was it?

361

How Can You Use Electricity Safely?

Plug in a toaster. Turn on the radio. Turn on the light. You use electric energy every day. Do you ever think much about it? Probably not.

Electric devices can be dangerous if they are not used properly. Knowing a few safety rules is important. They can help you make sure electricity doesn't pose a danger to you.

HEALTH
LINK

SAFETY RULE		REASON
• Never touch a wall socket with anything but a plug.		Current could flow from the socket to the item to you.
• Never touch the metal part of a plug when you plug it in.		Your finger could create a short-circuit path for the current.
• Never use a cord that is torn or has a hole in it.		You can create a short circuit.
• Don't pull the cord to remove a plug.		You can damage the plug or create a hole in the cord.
• Don't overload a plug or extension cord with too many devices.		Overloaded plugs draw too much current. They can get hot and cause a fire.
• Stay away from high-voltage cables and train rails.	WARNING HIGH VOLTAGE	You could accidentally touch them and be electrocuted.
• Never use electric devices when you are wet. Also do not use them if you are standing in or near water.		Water is a conductor. Therefore, you are a better conductor when wet. You can get a shock or be electrocuted.

Much of the energy we use is transformed, or changed, from one form into another.

We can cook food and heat our homes because electrical energy can be changed to heat energy. We can turn on a lamp because it can be changed to light energy. We can listen to tapes or CDs because it can be changed in part to sound energy. We can make a milk shake in the blender because it can be changed to mechanical energy. Knowing how to change energy from one form into another is a useful thing!

REVIEW

1. How was light energy transformed into heat energy in the Explore Activity?

2. Give an example of how electrical energy can be transformed into sound energy.

3. Give an example of how electrical energy can be transformed into light energy.

4. **COMMUNICATE** A friend is about to plug a fourth appliance into an extension cord. What would you tell her?

5. **CRITICAL THINKING** *Apply* A battery-operated toy has flashing lights and a siren, and it jumps up and down. Describe all the energy transformations that occur.

WHY IT MATTERS THINK ABOUT IT
How many different ways have you used transformed electrical energy in the past two days?

WHY IT MATTERS WRITE ABOUT IT
List some things you did today that used electrical energy. Write about how the electrical energy was transformed into another form of energy.

Science, Technology, and Society

a POWER-ful SUN!

A lot of our energy comes from fuels like oil, coal, and gas. One day we'll run out of them, but what can we do? Use energy from the Sun!

When the Sun heats air, it rises and cooler air rushes in to take its place. The Sun's energy is now wind energy! It can turn windmills that, in turn, can produce electrical energy!

The Sun also warms water. It rises and evaporates. Then it falls as rain or snow. Now the Sun's energy fills rivers. We can use this water to run generators that produce electricity!

Solar panels on houses collect the Sun's energy. It can warm a house and heat its water supply.

Special cells collect the Sun's energy and change it into electrical energy.

The more we use the Sun, the less we'll need other fuels, and the cleaner our air will be!

DISCUSSION STARTER

1. Could we have wind energy without solar energy? Why or why not?

2. Why is it important to use as much solar energy as possible?

To learn more about solar energy, visit *www.mhschool.com/science* and enter the keyword DAYSTAR.

*inter*NET CONNECTION

SCIENCE WORDS

alternating
   current p. 342
direct
   current p. 342
electromagnet
   p. 333
energy transfor-
   mation p. 354

generator p. 343
magnetic
   field p. 332
pole p. 330
radiate p. 354
transformer p. 346
volt p. 345

USING SCIENCE WORDS

Number a paper from 1 to 10. Fill in 1 to 5 with words from the list above.

1. Winding a wire in loops around an iron bar creates a(n) __?__.

2. A device that creates alternating current is a(n) __?__.

3. Light energy is able to __?__ from a lit bulb.

4. Current that travels in only one direction is __?__.

5. Electrical energy being transformed into sound energy is an example of a(n) __?__.

6–10. Pick five words from the list above that were not used in 1 to 5, and use each in a sentence.

UNDERSTANDING SCIENCE IDEAS

11. What are some uses for electromagnets?

12. What is a volt?

USING IDEAS AND SKILLS

13. **READING SKILL: CAUSE AND EFFECT** What happens when opposite poles of magnets are brought together? When the same poles are brought together? What causes this to happen?

14. **USE NUMBERS** Five 4-volt cells are connected. What do they make?

15. **THINKING LIKE A SCIENTIST** Think of a new use for an electric motor. How could you harness its energy to make a part of your life easier?

MATH
LINK

PROBLEMS and PUZZLES

Magnetic Strength How far away can a magnet be from an object it is trying to attract? Does it matter if there is paper, plastic, or wood between the object and the magnet? Design an experiment to test your ideas.

SCIENCE WORDS

conductor p. 295

discharge p. 295

electromagnet
  p. 333

energy transfor-
  mation p. 354

fuse p. 322

generator p. 343

insulator p. 295

open circuit p. 305

pole p. 330

radiate p. 354

resistor p. 307

series
  circuit p. 316

short circuit p. 308

static
  electricity p. 294

switch p. 309

transformer p. 346

volt p. 345

USING SCIENCE WORDS

Number a paper from 1 to 10. Beside each number write the word or words that best complete the sentence.

1. The unit measuring the force that makes negative charges flow is a(n) __?__.

2. A buildup of an electrical charge on an object, such as a balloon, is called __?__.

3. A material through which electricity flows easily is a(n) __?__.

4. You can use a(n) __?__ to open or close a circuit.

5. If electricity travels first through one light bulb and then through a second light bulb, the bulbs are part of a(n) __?__.

6. A material that restricts the flow of electricity is a(n) __?__.

7. A magnet has both a north and a south __?__.

8. A magnet made by an electric current flowing through a wire coiled around an iron rod is a(n) __?__.

9. A device that keeps too much electric current from flowing through wires is a(n) __?__.

10. Changing electric energy to heat energy is an example of a(n) __?__.

UNDERSTANDING SCIENCE IDEAS

Write 11 to 15. For each number write the letter for the best answer. You may wish to use the hints provided.

11. If two balloons are attracted to each other, they may
    a. both have positive charges
    b. both have negative charges
    c. have different charges
    d. have no charge
    (Hint: Read pages 292–293.)

12. Current electricity
    a. is positive
    b. flows through a circuit
    c. attracts balloons
    d. repels balloons
    (Hint: Read page 304.)

13. Light bulbs that are separately connected to the same cell are
    a. all on or all off
    b. on a series circuit
    c. on a parallel circuit
    d. on the same circuit
    (Hint: Read page 317.)

14. A compass points north because
    a. it is a magnet
    b. it is a closed circuit
    c. it has a generator
    d. it is made of metal
    (Hint: Read pages 331–332.)

15. Electrical energy can be changed
   a. into only light energy
   b. into only heat energy
   c. into only two forms of energy
   d. into many forms of energy
   (Hint: Read page 354.)

USING IDEAS AND SKILLS

16. Explain why lightning rods should be made of metal.

17. Draw a closed circuit that includes a cell, a light bulb, and a switch.

18. **PREDICT** You are using the computer. Your sister is listening to the radio. Your mother is using the blender. Your father turns on the vacuum cleaner. Suddenly all the lights go out. The appliances don't work. What do you think happened?

19. Explain how Earth's magnetic field affects magnets. Why is this important?

THINKING LIKE A SCIENTIST

20. **USE NUMBERS** What if a transformer changes an electrical force from 100 volts to 50 volts? How would the same transformer change an electrical force of 20 volts? Explain.

*inter*NET
CONNECTION

For help in reviewing this unit, visit
www.mhschool.com/science

WRITING IN YOUR JOURNAL

SCIENCE IN YOUR LIFE
Describe the two types of cells used to make electric current. What are some of the things you do that use electricity made by cells?

PRODUCT ADS
You may have seen advertisements for batteries (dry cells) that claim that this brand or that brand is the best. Explain what you think would make one kind of battery better than another kind. How could you find out which brand of battery is better?

HOW SCIENTISTS WORK
In this unit you learned that Joseph Henry made the first electric motor more than 100 years ago. In what ways do you think scientists today could try to transform electrical energy into mechanical energy?

Design your own
Experiment

You have a circuit with a switch and three light bulbs. Can you have two lights always lit and one light always off? Design an experiment to find out. Review your experiment with your teacher before testing your ideas.

PROBLEMS and PUZZLES

Body Power

Design a device that would use your own body power to light a light bulb. You can use any materials that appeared in this unit, or any others you wish. Build or draw a model.

ON AND OFF

Rewire this circuit so you can flip a switch to do one or two of these things:

1. Turn on both lights.
2. Turn off both lights.
3. Turn on A but not B.
4. Turn on B but not A.

Build or draw a model of your circuit. If possible, test your design.

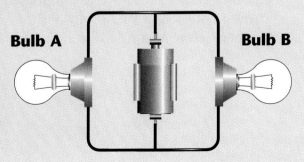

Bulb A   Bulb B

The EAT Mystery

THE PROBLEM

The EAT restaurant sign is made of 57 light bulbs. The sign works when all 57 bulbs are on. If one bulb burns out, the whole sign goes dark. When this happens, the manager needs to test each bulb—one at a time. Finding the burnt-out bulb takes a long time!

Your job is to change the system so one burnt-out bulb doesn't make the whole sign go dark. You should also make it easier for the manager to find the burnt-out bulb.

THE PLAN

Write a hypothesis that will help you solve the problem. Draw a diagram or make a model of the system.

TEST

Test your hypothesis. Explain how you would test your hypothesis. What would you expect to happen? How would you change your plan if it didn't work?

EVALUATE AND PUBLISH

How would you judge whether or not your plan worked?

Write a report in your *Science Journal*. Describe your plan in detail. Tell how you would test it.

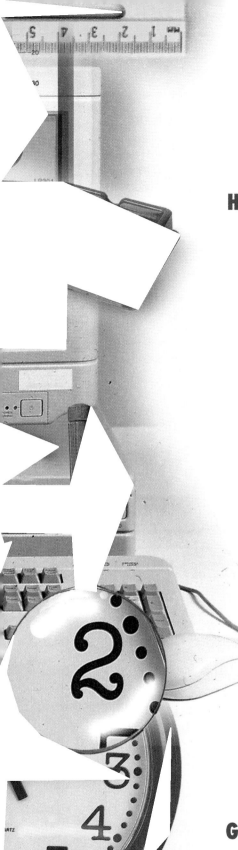

REFERENCE SECTION

HANDBOOK

Temperature

1. The temperature is 77 degrees Fahrenheit.

2. That is the same as 25 degrees Celsius.

3. Water boils at 212 degrees Fahrenheit.

4. Water freezes at 0 degrees Celsius.

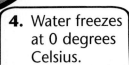

Length and Area

1. This classroom is 10 meters wide and 20 meters long.

2. That means the area is 200 square meters.

2. 32 ounces is the same as 2 pounds.

3. The mass of the bat is 907 grams.

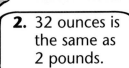

Mass and Weight

1. That baseball bat weighs 32 ounces.

Volume of Fluids

1. This bottle of juice has a volume of 1 liter.

2. That is a little more than 1 quart.

Weight/Force

I weigh 85 pounds. That is a force of 380.8 newtons.

Rate

1. She can walk 20 meters in 5 seconds.

2. That means her speed is 4 meters per second.

Table of Measurements

SI (International System) of Units	English System of Units
Temperature Water freezes at 0 degrees Celsius (°C) and boils at 100°C.	**Temperature** Water freezes at 32 degrees Fahrenheit (°F) and boils at 212°F.
Length and Distance 10 millimeters (mm) = 1 centimeter (cm) 100 centimeters = 1 meter (m) 1,000 meters = 1 kilometer (km)	**Length and Distance** 12 inches (in.) = 1 foot (ft) 3 feet = 1 yard (yd) 5,280 feet = 1 mile (mi)
Volume 1 cubic centimeter (cm^3) = 1 milliliter (mL) 1,000 milliliters = 1 liter (L)	**Volume of Fluids** 8 fluid ounces (fl oz) = 1 cup (c) 2 cups = 1 pint (pt) 2 pints = 1 quart (qt) 4 quarts = 1 gallon (gal)
Mass 1,000 milligrams (mg) = 1 gram (g) 1,000 grams = 1 kilogram (kg)	**Weight** 16 ounces (oz) = 1 pound (lb) 2,000 pounds = 1 ton (T)
Area 1 square kilometer (km^2) = l km x l km 1 hectare = 10,000 square meters (m^2)	**Rate** mph = miles per hour
Rate m/s = meters per second km/h = kilometers per hour	
Force 1 newton (N) = 1 kg x m/s^2	

In the Classroom

The most important part of doing any experiment is doing it safely. You can be safe by paying attention to your teacher and doing your work carefully. Here are some other ways to stay safe while you do experiments.

Before the Experiment

- Read all of the directions. Make sure you understand them. When you see ◤◤◤, be sure to follow the safety rule.
- Listen to your teacher for special safety directions. If you don't understand something, ask for help.
- Wash your hands with soap and water before an activity.

During the Experiment

- Wear safety goggles when your teacher tells you to wear them and whenever you see . Wear goggles when working with something that can fly into your eyes.
- Wear splash-proof goggles when working with liquids.
- Wear a safety apron if you work with anything messy or anything that might spill.

- If you spill something, wipe it up right away or ask your teacher for help.
- Tell your teacher if something breaks. If glass breaks do not clean it up yourself.
- Keep your hair and clothes away from open flames. Tie back long hair and roll up long sleeves.

- Be careful around a hot plate. Know when it is on and when it is off. Remember that the plate stays hot for a few minutes after you turn it off.
- Keep your hands dry around electrical equipment.
- Don't eat or drink anything during the experiment.

After the Experiment

- Put equipment back the way your teacher tells you.
- Dispose of things the way your teacher tells you.
- Clean up your work area and wash your hands with soap and water.

In the Field

- Always be accompanied by a trusted adult—like your teacher or a parent or guardian.
- Never touch animals or plants without the adult's approval. The animal might bite. The plant might be poison ivy or another dangerous plant.

Responsibility

Acting safely is one way to be responsible. You can also be responsible by treating animals, the environment, and each other with respect in the class and in the field.

Treat Living Things with Respect

- If you have animals in the classroom, keep their homes clean. Change the water in fish tanks and clean out cages.
- Feed classroom animals the right amounts of food.

- Give your classroom animals enough space.
- When you observe animals, don't hurt them or disturb their homes.
- Find a way to care for animals while school is on vacation.

Treat the Environment with Respect

- Do not pick flowers.
- Do not litter, including gum and food.
- If you see litter, ask your teacher if you can pick it up.

- Recycle materials used in experiments. Ask your teacher what materials can be recycled instead of thrown away. These might include plastics, aluminum, and newspapers.

Treat Each Other with Respect

- Use materials carefully around others so that people don't get hurt or get stains on their clothes.
- Be careful not to bump people when they are doing experiments. Do not disturb or damage their experiments.
- If you see that people are having trouble with an experiment, help them.

Use a Hand Lens

You use a hand lens to magnify an object, or make the object look larger. With a hand lens, you can see details that would be hard to see without the hand lens.

Magnify a Piece of Cereal

1. Place a piece of your favorite cereal on a flat surface. Look at the cereal carefully. Draw a picture of it.
2. Hold the hand lens so that it is just above the cereal. Look through the lens, and slowly move it away from the cereal. The cereal will look larger.
3. Keep moving the hand lens until the cereal begins to look blurry. Then move the lens a little closer to the cereal until you can see it clearly.
4. Draw a picture of the cereal as you see it through the hand lens. Fill in details that you did not see before.
5. Repeat this activity using objects you are studying in science. It might be a rock, some soil, a flower, a seed, or something else.

Use a Microscope

Hand lenses make objects look several times larger. A microscope, however, can magnify an object to look hundreds of times larger.

Examine Salt Grains

1. Place the microscope on a flat surface. Always carry a microscope with both hands. Hold the arm with one hand, and put your other hand beneath the base.
2. Look at the drawing to learn the different parts of the microscope.
3. Move the mirror so that it reflects light up toward the stage. Never point the mirror directly at the Sun or a bright light. Bright light can cause permanent eye damage.
4. Place a few grains of salt on the slide. Put the slide under the stage clips on the stage. Be sure that the salt grains are over the hole in the stage.
5. Look through the eyepiece. Turn the focusing knob slowly until the salt grains come into focus.
6. Draw what the grains look like through the microscope.
7. Look at other objects through the microscope. Try a piece of leaf, a strand of human hair, or a pencil mark.
8. Draw what each object looks like through the microscope. Do any of the objects look alike? If so, how? Are any of the objects alive? How do you know?

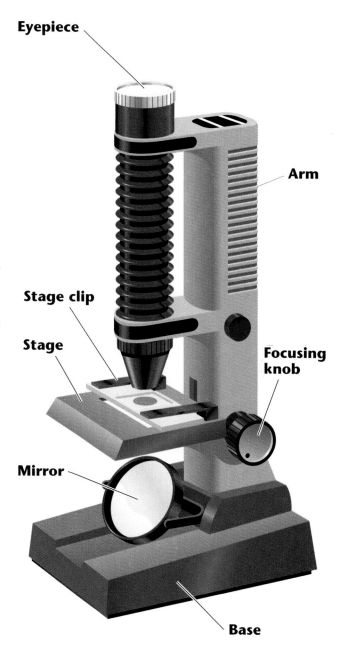

Eyepiece

Arm

Stage clip

Stage

Focusing knob

Mirror

Base

Use a Compass

HANDBOOK

You use a compass to find directions. A compass is a small, thin magnet that swings freely, like a spinner in a board game. One end of the magnet always points north. This end is the magnet's north pole. How does a compass work?

1. Place the compass on a surface that has no magnetic material such as steel. A wooden table or a sidewalk works well.
2. Find the magnet's north pole. The north pole is marked in some way, usually with a color or an arrowhead.
3. Notice the letters *N, E, S,* and *W* on the compass. These letters stand for the directions north, east, south, and west. When the magnet stops swinging, turn the compass so that the *N* lines up with the north pole of the magnet.
4. Face to the north. Then face to the east, to the south, and to the west.
5. Repeat this activity by holding the compass in your hand and then at different places indoors and outdoors.

Use a Compass to Study Shadows

A shadow is the shade that something makes when that thing blocks light. A shadow points away from the light that causes it. Find out how shadows change as the Sun moves across the sky.

1. Go outside on a sunny morning, and look at your shadow. Hold a compass flat in the palm of your hand. In which direction is your shadow pointing? In which direction is the Sun in the sky?
2. Go outside late in the afternoon with the compass. Now in which direction is your shadow pointing? In which direction is the Sun in the sky?

Use a Telescope

Have you ever seen the Moon near the horizon? A little while later, the Moon is higher in the sky. The Moon appears to move across the sky because Earth turns. Do stars appear to move across the sky, too? Make these observations on a clear night to find out.

Look at the Stars

1. Pick out a group of stars that you would be able to find again. The Big Dipper is a good choice. Choose a star in the star group.
2. Notice where the star is located compared to a treetop, a house roof, or some other point on land.
3. Find the same star an hour later. Notice that it appears to have moved in the sky. Predict how far the star will appear to move in another hour. Observe the star in an hour to check your prediction.

A telescope gathers light better than your eyes can. With a telescope you can see stars that you could not see with just your eyes.

The Moon moves around Earth. As a result of this motion, different parts of the Moon are lit by the Sun at different times. The Moon looks like it changes shape. These shapes are the Moon's phases. It takes about 30 days for the Moon to make one trip around Earth and complete all its phases. Check this out for yourself.

Look at the Moon

1. Make a calendar that shows the next 30 days.
2. Each day draw in the Moon's shape in the calendar box for that day. How many days does it take to come back to the same shape?

Use a Camera, Tape Recorder, Map, and Compass

HANDBOOK

Camera

You can use a camera to record what you observe in nature. Keep these tips in mind.

1. Hold the camera steady. Gently press the button so that you do not jerk the camera.
2. Try to take pictures with the Sun at your back. Then your pictures will be bright and clear.
3. Don't get too close to the subject. Without a special lens, the picture could turn out blurry.
4. Be patient. If you are taking a picture of an animal, you may have to wait for the animal to appear.

Tape Recorder

You can record observations on a tape recorder. This is sometimes better than writing notes because a tape recorder can record your observations at the exact time you are making them. Later you can listen to the tape and write down your observations.

Map and Compass

When you are busy observing nature, it might be easy to get lost. You can use a map of the area and a compass to find your way. Here are some tips.

1. Lightly mark on the map your starting place. It might be the place where the bus parked.
2. Always know where you are on the map compared to your starting place. Watch for landmarks on the map, such as a river, a pond, trails, or buildings.
3. Use the map and compass to find special places to observe, such as a pond. Look at the map to see which direction the place is from you. Hold the compass to see where that direction is.
4. Use your map and compass with a friend.

Length

Find Length with a Ruler

1. Look at this section of a ruler. Each centimeter is divided into 10 millimeters. How long is the paper clip?
2. The length of the paper clip is 3 centimeters plus 2 millimeters. You can write this length as 3.2 centimeters.
3. Place the ruler on your desk. Lay a pencil against the ruler so that one end of the pencil lines up with the left edge of the ruler. Record the length of the pencil.
4. Trade your pencil with a classmate. Measure and record the length of each other's pencils. Compare your answers.

Measuring Area

Area is the amount of surface something covers. To find the area of a rectangle, multiply the rectangle's length by its width. For example, the rectangle here is 3 centimeters long and 2 centimeters wide. Its area is 3 cm x 2 cm = 6 square centimeters. You write the area as 6 cm².

1. Find the area of your science book. Measure the book's length to the nearest centimeter. Measure its width.
2. Multiply the book's length by its width. Remember to put the answer in cm².

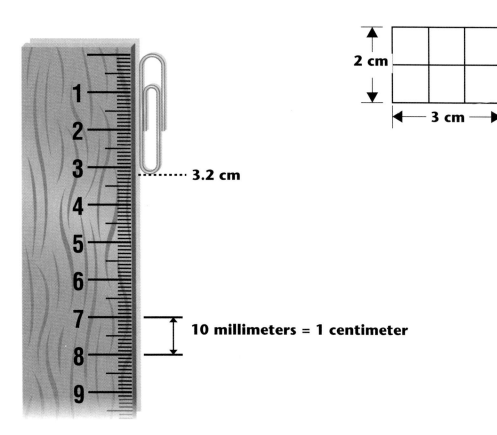

3.2 cm

10 millimeters = 1 centimeter

2 cm

3 cm

Time

You use timing devices to measure how long something takes to happen. Some timing devices you use in science are a clock with a second hand and a stopwatch. Which one is more accurate?

Comparing a Clock and a Stopwatch

1. Look at a clock with a second hand. The second hand is the hand that you can see moving. It measures seconds.
2. Get an egg timer with falling sand or some device like a windup toy that runs down after a certain length of time. When the second hand of the clock points to 12, tell your partner to start the egg timer. Watch the clock while the sand in the egg timer is falling.
3. When the sand stops falling, count how many seconds it took. Record this measurement. Repeat the activity, and compare the two measurements.
4. Switch roles with your partner.
5. Look at a stopwatch. Click the button on the top right. This starts the time. Click the button again. This stops the time. Click the button on the top left. This sets the stopwatch back to zero. Notice that the stopwatch tells time in hours, minutes, seconds, and hundredths of a second.
6. Repeat the activity in steps 1–3, but use the stopwatch instead of a clock. Make sure the stopwatch is set to zero. Click the top right button to start timing.

Click the button again when the sand stops falling. Make sure you and your partner time the sand twice.

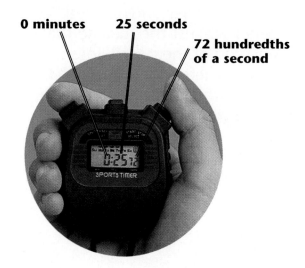

0 minutes   25 seconds

72 hundredths of a second

More About Time

1. Use the stopwatch to time how long it takes an ice cube to melt under cold running water. How long does an ice cube take to melt under warm running water?
2. Match each of these times with the action you think took that amount of time.

a.   b.   c.

1. A Little League baseball game
2. Saying the Pledge of Allegiance
3. Recess

Volume

Have you ever used a measuring cup? Measuring cups measure the volume of liquids. Volume is the amount of space something takes up. To bake a cake, you might measure the volume of water, vegetable oil, or melted butter. In science you use special measuring cups called beakers and graduated cylinders. These containers are marked in milliliters (mL).

Measure the Volume of a Liquid

1. Look at the beaker and at the graduated cylinder. The beaker has marks for each 25 mL up to 200 mL. The graduated cylinder has marks for each 1 mL up to 100 mL.

2. The surface of the water in the graduated cylinder curves up at the sides. You measure the volume by reading the height of the water at the flat part. What is the volume of water in the graduated cylinder? How much water is in the beaker? They both contain 75 mL of water.

3. Pour 50 mL of water from a pitcher into a graduated cylinder. The water should be at the 50-mL mark on the graduated cylinder. If you go over the mark, pour a little water back into the pitcher.

4. Pour the 50 mL of water into a beaker.

5. Repeat steps 3 and 4 using 30 mL, 45 mL, and 25 mL of water.

6. Measure the volume of water you have in the beaker. Do you have about the same amount of water as your classmates?

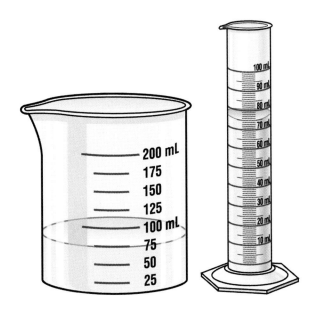

Mass

Mass is the amount of matter an object has. You use a balance to measure mass. To find the mass of an object, you balance it with objects whose masses you know. Let's find the mass of a box of crayons.

Measure the Mass of a Box of Crayons

1. Place the balance on a flat, level surface. Check that the two pans are empty and clean.
2. Make sure the empty pans are balanced with each other. The pointer should point to the middle mark. If it does not, move the slider a little to the right or left to balance the pans.

3. Gently place a box of crayons on the left pan. This pan will drop lower.
4. Add masses to the right pan until the pans are balanced.
5. Add the numbers on the masses that are in the right pan. The total is the mass of the box of crayons, in grams. Record this number. After the number, write a *g* for "grams."

Predict the Mass of More Crayons

1. Leave the box of crayons and the masses on the balance.
2. Get two more crayons. If you put them in the pan with the box of crayons, what do you think the mass of all the crayons will be? Write down what you predict the total mass will be.
3. Check your prediction. Gently place the two crayons in the left pan. Add masses to the right pan until the pans are balanced.
4. Add the numbers on the masses as you did before. Record this number. How close is it to your prediction?

More About Mass

What was the mass of all your crayons? It was probably less than 100 grams. What would happen if you replaced the crayons with a pineapple? You may not have enough masses to balance the pineapple. It has a mass of about 1,000 grams. That's the same as 1 kilogram because *kilo* means "1,000."

1. How many kilograms do all these masses add up to?

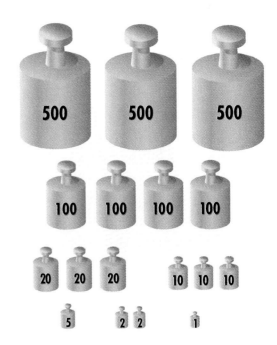

2. Which of these objects have a mass greater than 1 kilogram?
   a. large dog
   b. robin
   c. desktop computer
   d. calculator
   e. whole watermelon

Weight/Force

You use a spring scale to measure weight. An object has weight because the force of gravity pulls down on the object. Therefore, weight is a force. Like all forces weight is measured in newtons (N).

Measure the Weight of an Object

1. Look at your spring scale to see how many newtons it measures. See how the measurements are divided. The spring scale shown here measures up to 10 N. It has a mark for every 1 N.
2. Hold the spring scale by the top loop. Put the object to be measured on the bottom hook. If the object will not stay on the hook, place it in a net bag. Then hang the bag from the hook.
3. Let go of the object slowly. It will pull down on a spring inside the scale. The spring is connected to a pointer. The pointer on the spring scale shown here is a small arrow.

4. Wait for the pointer to stop moving. Read the number of newtons next to the pointer. This is the object's weight. The mug in the picture weighs 3 N.

More About Spring Scales

You probably weigh yourself by standing on a bathroom scale. This is a spring scale. The force of your body stretches a spring inside the scale. The dial on the scale is probably marked in pounds—the English unit of weight. One pound is equal to about 4.5 newtons.

Here are some spring scales you may have seen.

Temperature

Temperature is how hot or cold something is. You use a thermometer to measure temperature. A thermometer is made of a thin tube with colored liquid inside. When the liquid gets warmer, it expands and moves up the tube. When the liquid gets cooler, it contracts and moves down the tube. You may have seen most temperatures measured in degrees Fahrenheit (°F). Scientists measure temperature in degrees Celsius (°C).

Read a Thermometer

1. Look at the thermometer shown here. It has two scales—a Fahrenheit scale and a Celsius scale. Every 20 degrees on each scale has a number.

2. What is the temperature shown on the thermometer? At what temperature does water freeze? Give your answers in °F and in °C.

How Is Temperature Measured?

1. Fill a large beaker about one-half full of cool water. Find the temperature of the water by holding a thermometer in the water. Do not let the bulb at the bottom of the thermometer touch the sides or bottom of the beaker.

2. Keep the thermometer in the water until the liquid in the tube stops moving—about a minute. Read and record the temperature on the Celsius scale.

3. Fill another large beaker one-half full of warm water from a faucet. Be careful not to burn yourself by using hot water.

4. Find and record the temperature of the warm water just as you did in steps 1 and 2.

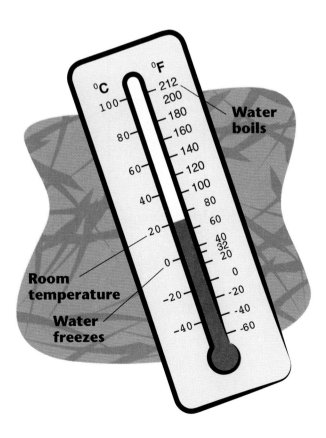

Weather

What was the weather like yesterday? What is it like today? The weather changes from day to day. You can observe different parts of the weather to find out how it changes.

Measure Temperature

1. Use a thermometer to find the air temperature outside. Look at page R17 to review thermometers.
2. Hold a thermometer outside for two minutes. Then read and record the temperature.
3. Take the temperature at the same time each day for a week. Record it in a chart.

Observe Wind Speed and Direction

1. Observe how the wind is affecting things around you. Look at a flag or the branches of a tree. How hard is the wind blowing the flag or branches? Observe for about five minutes. Write down your observations.
2. Hold a compass to see which direction the wind is coming from. Write down this direction.
3. Observe the wind each day for a week. Record your observations in your chart.

Observe Clouds, Rain, and Snow

1. Observe how much of the sky is covered by clouds. Use these symbols to record the cloud cover in your chart each day.

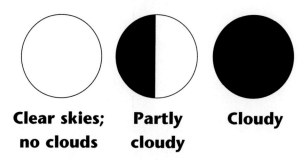

Clear skies; no clouds   **Partly cloudy**   **Cloudy**

2. Record in your chart if it is raining or snowing.
3. At the end of the week, how has the weather changed from day to day?

MONDAY	TUESDAY	WEDNESDAY
25°C Strong winds from south ● Rain	23°C Light wind	

Systems

What do a toy car, a tomato plant, and a yo-yo have in common? They are all systems. A system is a set of parts that work together to form a whole. Look at the three systems below. Think of how each part helps the system work.

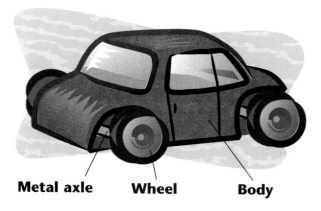

Metal axle   **Wheel**   **Body**

This system has three main parts—the body, the axles, and the wheels. Would the system work well if the axles could not turn?

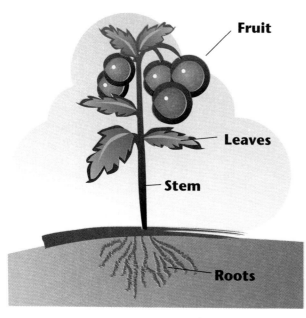

Fruit

Leaves

Stem

Roots

In this system roots take in water, and leaves make food. The stem carries water and food to different parts of the plant. What would happen if you cut off all the leaves?

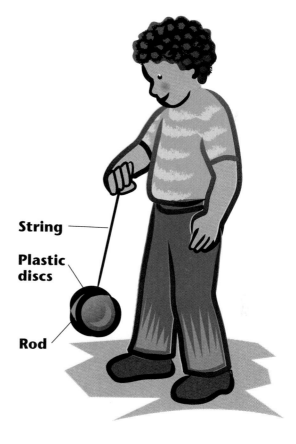

String

Plastic discs

Rod

Even simple things can be systems. How do all the parts of the yo-yo work together to make the toy go up and down?

Look for some other systems at school, at home, and outside. Remember to look for things that are made of parts. List the parts. Then describe how you think each part helps the system work.

Make Graphs to Organize Data

When you do an experiment in science, you collect information. To find out what your information means, you can organize it into graphs. There are many kinds of graphs.

Bar Graphs

A bar graph uses bars to show information. For example, suppose you are growing a plant. Every week you measure how high the plant has grown. Here is what you find.

Week	Height (cm)
1	1
2	3
3	6
4	10
5	17
6	20
7	22
8	23

The bar graph at right organizes the measurements you collected so that you can easily compare them.

1. Look at the bar for week 2. Put your finger at the top of the bar. Move your finger straight over to the left to find how many centimeters the plant grew by the end of week 2.
2. Between which two weeks did the plant grow most?
3. When did plant growth begin to level off?

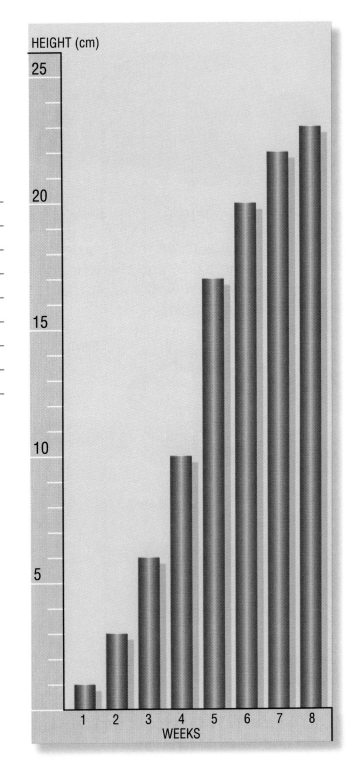

Pictographs

A pictograph uses symbols, or pictures, to show information. What if you collect information about how much water your family uses each day? Here is what you find.

Activity	Water Used Each Day (L)
Drinking	10
Showering	180
Bathing	240
Brushing teeth	80
Washing dishes	140
Washing hands	30
Washing clothes	280
Flushing toilet	90

You can organize this information into the pictograph shown here. The pictograph has to explain what the symbol on the graph means. In this case each bottle means 20 liters of water. A half bottle means half of 20, or 10 liters of water.

1. Which activity uses the most water?
2. Which activity uses the least water?

Line Graphs

A line graph shows information by connecting dots plotted on the graph.

It shows change over time. For example, what if you measure the temperature out of doors every hour starting at 6 A.M.? Here is what you find.

Time	Temperature (°C)
6 A.M.	10
7 A.M.	12
8 A.M.	14
9 A.M.	16
10 A.M.	18
11 A.M.	20

You can organize this information into a line graph. Follow these steps.

1. Make a scale along the bottom and side of the graph. The scales should include all the numbers in the chart. Label the scales.
2. Plot points on the graph. For example, place your finger at the "6 A.M." on the bottom line. Place a finger from your other hand on the "10" on the left line. Move your "6 A.M." finger up and your "10" finger to the right until they meet, and make a pencil point. Plot the other points in this way.
3. Connect the points with a line.

A Family's Daily Use of Water

Make Maps to Show Information

Locate Places

A map is a drawing that shows an area from above. Most maps have numbers and letters along the top and side. They help you find places easily. For example, what if you wanted to find the library on the map below. It is located at D7. Place a finger on the letter D along the side of the map and another finger on the number 7 at the top. Then move your fingers straight across and down the map until they meet. The library is located where D and 7 meet, or very nearby.

1. What building is located at G3?
2. The hospital is located three blocks south and three blocks east of the library. What is its number and letter?
3. Make a map of an area in your community. It might be a park or the area between your home and school. Include numbers and letters along the top and side. Use a compass to find north, and mark north on your map. Exchange maps with classmates.

Idea Maps

The map below left shows how places are connected to each other. Idea maps, on the other hand, show how ideas are connected to each other. Idea maps help you organize information about a topic.

Look at the idea map below. It connects ideas about water. This map shows that Earth's water is either fresh water or salt water. The map also shows four sources of fresh water. You can see that there is no connection between "rivers" and "salt water" on the map. This reminds you that salt water does not flow in rivers.

Make an idea map about a topic you are learning in science. Your map can include words, phrases, or even sentences. Arrange your map in a way that makes sense to you and helps you understand the ideas.

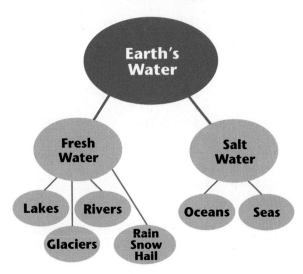

HANDBOOK

Make Tables and Charts to Organize Data

Tables help you organize data during experiments. Most tables have columns that run up and down, and rows that run across. The columns and rows have headings that tell you what kind of data goes in each part of the table.

A Sample Table

What if you are going to do an experiment to find out how long different kinds of seeds take to sprout? Before you begin the experiment, you should set up your table. Follow these steps.

1. In this experiment you will plant 20 radish seeds, 20 bean seeds, and 20 corn seeds. Your table must show how many of each kind of seed sprouted on days 1, 2, 3, 4, and 5.
2. Make your table with columns, rows, and headings. You might use a computer. Some computer programs let you build a table with just the click of a mouse. You can delete or add columns and rows if you need to.
3. Give your table a title. Your table could look like the one here.

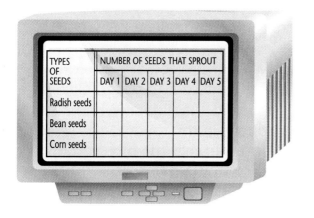

TYPES OF SEEDS	NUMBER OF SEEDS THAT SPROUT				
	DAY 1	DAY 2	DAY 3	DAY 4	DAY 5
Radish seeds					
Bean seeds					
Corn seeds					

Make a Table

Now what if you are going to do an experiment to find out how temperature affects the sprouting of seeds? You will plant 20 bean seeds in each of two trays. You will keep each tray at a different temperature, as shown below, and observe the trays for seven days. Make a table that you can use for this experiment. You can use the table to record, examine, and evaluate the information of this experiment.

Make a Chart

A chart is simply a table with pictures as well as words to label the rows or columns. Make a chart that shows the information of the above experiment.

R23

Computer

A computer has many uses. The Internet connects your computer to many other computers around the world, so you can collect all kinds of information. You can use a computer to show this information and write reports. Best of all you can use a computer to explore, discover, and learn.

You can also get information from CD-ROMs. They are computer disks that can hold large amounts of information. You can fit a whole encyclopedia on one CD-ROM.

Use Computers for a Project

Here is how one group of students uses computers as they work on a weather project.

1. The students use instruments to measure temperature, wind speed, wind direction, and other parts of the weather. They input this information, or data, into the computer. The students keep the data in a table. This helps them compare the data from one day to the next.

2. The teacher finds out that another group of students in a town 200 kilometers to the west is also doing a weather project. The two groups use the Internet to talk to each other and share data. When a storm happens in the town to the west, that group tells the other group that it's coming its way.

email: It's going to storm here. The sky is turning dark gray. The winds are sometimes 65 km per hour from the northwest.

3. The students want to find out more. They decide to stay on the Internet and send questions to a local TV weather forecaster. She has a Web site and answers questions from students every day.

4. Meanwhile some students go to the library to gather more information from a CD-ROM disk. The CD-ROM has an encyclopedia that includes movie clips with sound. The clips give examples of different kinds of storms.

5. The students have kept all their information in a folder called Weather Project. Now they use that information to write a report about the weather. On the computer they can move paragraphs, add words, take out words, put in diagrams, and draw their own weather maps. Then they print the report in color.

6. Use the information on these two pages to plan your own investigation. You can study the weather. Use a computer, Internet, CD-ROM, or any other technological device.

Calculator

Sometimes after you make measurements, you have to multiply or divide your measurements to get other information. A calculator helps you multiply and divide, especially if the numbers have decimal points.

Multiply Decimals

What if you are measuring the width of your classroom? You discover that the floor is covered with tiles and the room is exactly 32 tiles wide. You measure a tile, and it is 22.7 centimeters wide. To find the width of the room, you can multiply 32 by 22.7. You can use your calculator.

1. Make sure the calculator is on. Press the **ON** key.

2. Press **3** and **2**.

3. Press **×**.

4. Press **2**, **2**, **.**, and **7**.

5. Press **=**. Your total should be 726.4. That is how wide the room is in centimeters.

Divide Decimals

Now what if you wanted to find out how many desks placed side by side would be needed to reach across the room? You measure one desk, and it is 60 centimeters wide. To find the number of desks needed, divide 726.4 by 60.

1. Turn the calculator on.
2. Press **7**, **2**, **6**, **.**, and **4**.
3. Press **÷**.
4. Press **6** and **0**.
5. Press **=**. Your total should be about 12.1. This means you can fit 12 desks across the room with a little space left over.

What if the room was 35 tiles wide? How wide would the room be? How many desks would fit across it?

GLOSSARY

This Glossary will help you to pronounce and understand the meanings of the Science Words introduced in this book. The page number at the end of the definition tells where the word appears.

A

abuse (*v.*, ə būz′; *n.*, ə būs′) To use legal drugs in an unsafe way on purpose or to use illegal drugs. (p. 474)

adaptation (ad′əp tā′shən) A special trait that helps an organism survive. (p. 276)

addictive (ə dik′tiv) Causing dependence, or a strong need to have a particular substance. (p. 460)

alcohol (al′kə hôl′) A drug found in beer, wine, liquor, and even some medications. (p. 458)

allergy (al′ər jē) A sensitivity to a substance that can cause a rash, fever, or trouble breathing. (p. 471)

alloy (al′oi) A mixture of two or more metals. (p. 96)

alternating current (ôl′tər nā ting kûr′ənt) Current that flows in a circuit first in one direction, then in the opposite direction. (p. 342)

amber (am′bər) Hardened tree sap, yellow to brown in color, often a source of insect fossils. (p. 164)

amphibian (am fib′ē ən) A cold-blooded vertebrate that spends part of its life in water and part of its life on land. (p. 239)

antibiotic (an′tē bī ot′ik) A type of medicine that kills bacteria or stops them from growing. (p. 470)

area (âr′ē ə) The number of unit squares that fit inside a surface. (p. 81)

arthropod (är′thrə pod′) An invertebrate with jointed legs and a body that is divided into sections. (p. 227)

asexual reproduction (a sek′shü əl rē′prə duk′shən) Producing offspring with only one parent. (p. 268)

atmosphere (at′məs fîr′) Gases that surround Earth. (p. 372)

atom (at′əm) The smallest particle of an element that has all the properties of that element. (p. 88)

B

bacteria (bak tîr′ē ə) *pl.*, *sing.* **bacterium** (bak tîr′ē əm) One-celled organisms that have cell walls but no nuclei. (p. 19)

balance (bal′əns) An instrument used to measure mass. (p. 70)

biceps (bī′seps) A muscle in the upper arm that bends the arm by contracting. (p. 446)

bilateral symmetry (bī lat′ər əl sim′ə trē) A form of symmetry in which an animal has only two sides, which are mirror images. (p. 215)

bladder (blad′ər) The body structure that stores urine until it is removed from the body. (p. 254)

PRONUNCIATION KEY

a	at	e	end	o	hot	u	up	hw	white	ə	about
ā	ape	ē	me	ō	old	ū	use	ng	song		taken
ä	far	i	it	ô	fork	ü	rule	th	thin		pencil
âr	care	ī	ice	oi	oil	u̇	pull	t͟h	this		lemon
		îr	pierce	ou	out	ûr	turn	zh	measure		circus

′ = *primary accent; shows which syllable takes the main stress, such as* **kil** *in* **kilogram** (kil′ə gram′)

′ = *secondary accent; shows which syllables take lighter stresses, such as* **gram** *in* **kilogram**

budding (bud′ing) A form of asexual reproduction in simple invertebrates where a bud forms on the adult's body and slowly develops into a new animal before breaking off. (p. 268)

buoyancy (boi′ən sē) The upward force of a liquid or gas. (p. 69)

C

caffeine (ka fēn′) A stimulant found in tea, coffee, and many soft drinks. (p. 472)

camouflage (kam′ə fläzh′) An adaptation by which an animal can hide by blending in with its surroundings. (p. 276)

carbon monoxide (kär′bən mon ok′sīd) A poisonous gas given off by burning tobacco. (p. 462)

cardiac muscle (kär′dē ak′ mus′əl) The type of muscle that makes up the heart. (p. 448)

carnivore (kär′nə vôr′) A consumer that eats only animals. (p. 56)

cartilage (kär′tə lij) A flexible tissue that covers the ends of some bones; found in the nose and ears. (p. 439)

cartilaginous (kär′tə laj′ə nəs) Said of a fish with a skeleton made of cartilage. (p. 237)

cast (kast) A fossil formed or shaped within a mold. (p. 163)

cell (sel) The smallest unit of living matter. (p. 5)

cell membrane (sel mem′brān) An animal cell's thin outer covering. It is found beneath the cell wall in plants. (p. 15)

cell wall (sel wôl) A thick, stiff structure that protects and supports a plant cell. (p. 14)

chemical change (kem′i kəl chānj) A change that produces new matter with different properties from the original matter. *See* **physical change**. (p. 104)

chitin (kī′tin) A light but tough material that makes up the exoskeletons of certain invertebrates. (p. 228)

chlorophyll (klôr′ə fil′) A material (usually green) found in plant cells that makes food for the plant when sunlight strikes it. (p. 5)

chloroplast (klôr′ə plast′) A plant cell's food factory. Chloroplasts contain a substance (usually green) that uses the Sun's energy to make food. (p. 14)

chromosome (krō′mə sōm′) One of the threadlike structures inside a cell nucleus that determine an organism's traits. (p. 16)

circuit (sûr′kit) A complete path that electricity can move through. (p. 304)

circuit breaker (sûr′kit brā′kər) A reusable switch that protects circuits from dangerously high currents. (p. 322)

circulatory system (sûr′kyə lə tôr′ē sis′təm) The organ system that moves blood through the body. (p. 252)

class (klas) A smaller group within a phylum, such as all those animals that produce milk for their young. Classes are made up of smaller groups called *orders*. (p. 30)

clone (klōn) An exact copy of its parent formed by asexual reproduction. (p. 268)

closed circuit (klōzd sûr′kit) A clear and complete path that electricity can flow through. (p. 305)

cloud (kloud) Tiny drops of condensed water that gather in the atmosphere. (p. 385)

cnidarian (nī dâr′ē ən) An invertebrate with poison stingers on tentacles. (p. 223)

cocaine (kō kān′) An illegal stimulant made from the leaves of the coca plant. (p. 473)

cold-blooded (kōld′blud′id) Said of an animal that cannot control its body temperature. (p. 236)

community (kə mū′ni tē) The living part of an ecosystem. (p. 50)

compound (kom′pound) A substance made when two or more elements are joined and lose their own properties. (p. 94)

compound machine (kom′pound mə shēn′) A combination of two or more machines. (p. 139)

condensation (kon′den sā′shən) When water particles change from a gas to a liquid. (p. 385)

conduction (kən duk′shən) The transfer of energy caused by one particle of matter hitting into another. (p. 118)

conductor (kən duk′tər) 1. A material that transfers heat well. (p. 116) 2. Said of a material through which electricity flows easily. (p. 295)

consumer (kən sü′mər) Any organism that eats the food producers make. (p. 54)

continental glacier (kon′tə nen′təl glā′shər) A glacier covering large sections of land in Earth's polar regions. (p. 177)

contract (v., kən trakt′) To decrease in size, or shrink, as most matter does when it cools. (p. 120)

convection (kən′vek′shən) The transfer of energy by the flow of liquids or gases, such as water boiling in a pot or warm air rising in a room. (p. 118)

crack (krak) A very harmful form of cocaine. (p. 473)

crust (krust) Solid rock that makes up Earth's outermost layer. (p. 202)

crystal (kris′təl) The clear and shiny particle of frozen water that makes up a snowflake. (p. 390)

current (kûr′ənt) An ocean movement; a large stream of water that flows in the ocean. (p. 396)

current electricity (kûr′ənt i lek tris′i tē) A moving electrical charge. (p. 304)

cytoplasm (sī′tə plaz′əm) A jellylike substance that fills a cell. (p. 15)

D

decomposer (dē′kəm pō′zər) An organism that breaks down wastes and the remains of other organisms. (p. 54)

deep ocean current (dēp ō′shən kûr′ənt) A stream of water that flows more than 200 meters (650 feet) beneath the sea. (p. 396)

density (den′si tē) The amount of matter in a given space. In scientific terms density is the mass per unit of volume. (p. 84)

dependence (di pen′dəns) A strong need or desire for a medicine or drug. (p. 471)

depressant (di pres′ənt) A drug that slows down the activity of the body. (p. 459)

diaphragm (dī′ə fram′) A muscle below the lungs. When relaxed the diaphragm pushes up. Air leaves the lungs. When the diaphragm flattens and pulls down, the lungs fill with air. (p. 253)

digestive system (di jes′tiv sis′təm) The organ system that breaks down food for fuel. (p. 255)

direct current (di rekt′ kûr′ənt) Current that flows in one direction through a circuit. (p. 342)

discharge (v., dis chärj′; n., dis′chärj) When a buildup of electrical charge empties into something. (p. 295)

drought (drout) A long period of time with little or no precipitation. (p. 412)

drug (drug) A substance other than food that changes the way a person feels, thinks, and acts. (p. 458)

drumlin (drum′lin) An oval mound of glacial till. (p. 177)

GLOSSARY

PRONUNCIATION KEY

a at; ā ape; ä far; âr care; e end; ē me; i it; ī ice; îr pierce; o hot; ō old; ô fork; oi oil; ou out; u up; ū use;
ü rule; ů pull; ûr turn; hw white; ng song; th thin; <u>th</u> this; zh measure; ə about, taken, pencil, lemon, circus

dry cell (drī sel) A battery that changes chemical energy into electrical energy. It is made of a carbon rod and a moist chemical paste. (p. 306)

E

earthquake (ûrth′kwāk′) Movement or vibration in the rocks that make up Earth's crust. (p. 198)

echinoderm (i kī′nə dûrm′) A spiny-skinned invertebrate. (p. 226)

ecology (ē kol′ə jē) The study of how living and nonliving things interact. (p. 50)

ecosystem (ek′ō sis′təm) The living and nonliving things in an environment and all their interactions. (p. 50)

effort force (ef′ərt fôrs) The force applied to a machine. (p. 132)

egg (eg) The female sex cell. (p. 269)

electrical charge (i lek′tri kəl chärj) The positive or negative property of the particles that make up matter. (p. 292)

electricity (i lek tris′i tē) The energy caused by the flow of particles with negative electrical charges. (p. 292)

electrode (i lek′trōd) The negative or positive terminal of a wet cell. (p. 344)

electromagnet (i lek′trō mag′nit) A temporary magnet created when current flows through wire wrapped in coils around an iron bar. (p. 333)

element (el′ə mənt) A substance that is made up of only one type of matter. (p. 90)

embryo (em′brē ō′) A developing organism that results from fertilization; an undeveloped animal or plant. (pp. 43, 269)

endoskeleton (en′dō skel′i tən) An internal supporting structure. (p. 226)

energy (en′ər jē) The ability to do work. (p. 129)

energy transformation (en′ər jē trans′fər mā′shən) A change of energy from one form to another. (p. 354)

erosion (i rō′zhən) The wearing away of rocks and rock materials, as when glaciers leave distinctive features on Earth's surface. (p. 155)

erratic (i rat′ik) An isolated boulder left behind by a glacier. (p. 179)

evaporation (i vap′ə rā′shən) The change of a liquid to a gas. (pp. 93, 384)

evolution (ev′ə lü′shən) The change in living things over time. (p. 40)

excretory system (ek′skri tôr′ē sis′təm) The organ system that removes liquid wastes. (p. 254)

exoskeleton (ek′sō skel′i tən) A hard covering that protects the body of certain invertebrates. (p. 227)

expand (ek spand′) To swell or get larger, as most matter does when it is heated. (p. 120)

expiration date (ek′spə rā′shən dāt) The date on a medicine label after which the medicine should not be used. (p. 470)

extinct (ek stingkt′) Said of an organism no longer alive on Earth. (p. 43)

F

family (fam′ə lē) A smaller group of organisms within a class. Families are made up of still smaller groups of very similar organisms called *genuses*. (p. 30)

fault (fôlt) A break in Earth's outer layer caused by the movement of rocks. (p. 200)

fertilization (fûr′tə lə zā′shən) Occurs during sexual reproduction when an egg and a sperm join. (p. 269)

fertilizer (fûr′tə lī′zər) Chemicals or animal waste used to treat the soil so that plants grow stronger. (p. 423)

filter (fil′tər) A tool used to separate things by size. It works by means of an interwoven material that retains the bigger pieces but allows smaller pieces to fall through the holes of the filter. (p. 93)

filtration (fil trā′shən) The passing of a liquid through materials that remove solid impurities. (p. 424)

fixed pulley (fikst pùl′ē) A pulley that does not increase the effort force needed to move an object but does change the direction of that force. The pulley wheel is attached to one place so that the object moves, not the wheel. *See* **pulley**. (p. 134)

food chain (füd chān) The set of steps in which organisms get the food they need to survive. (p. 48)

food web (füd web) The pattern that shows how food chains are related. (p. 48)

force (fôrs) The push or pull needed to make an object move. (p. 128)

fossil (fos′əl) Any evidence of an organism that lived in the past. (pp. 40, 156)

fracture (frak′chər) A break or crack in a bone. (p. 439)

freeze (frēz) When moving particles in water slow down, lose heat, and change from a liquid to a solid. (p. 387)

fungi (fun′jī) *pl., sing.* **fungus** (fung′gəs) One- or many-celled organisms that lack true roots, stems, and leaves, and absorb food from dead organisms. (p. 19)

fuse (fūz) A device that melts to keep too much electric current from flowing through wires. Once melted a fuse cannot be reused. (p. 322)

G

gas (gas) A form of matter that does not take up a definite amount of space and has no definite shape. (p. 71)

gears (gîrz) Wheels with teeth that transfer motion and force from one source to another. (pp. 138, 358)

generator (jen′ər rā′tər) A device that creates alternating current by spinning an electric coil between the poles of a powerful magnet. (p. 343)

genus (jē′nəs) A group made up of two or more very similar species, like dogs and wolves. (p. 33)

geologist (jē ol′ə jist) A scientist who studies the physical properties of rocks to tell how the rocks may have formed. (p. 148)

gizzard (giz′ərd) A muscular organ in birds that breaks down food by grinding it with stored pebbles. (p. 255)

glacial till (glā′shəl til) An unsorted mixture of rock materials deposited as a glacier melts. (p. 177)

glacier (glā′shər) A large mass of ice and snow that moves over land. (pp. 176, 373)

grounded (ground′əd) Said of an electric charge that flows into the ground, or surface of Earth. (p. 297)

groundwater (ground wô′tər) Water stored in the cracks of underground rocks. (p. 374)

H

habitat (hab′i tat′) The home of an organism. (p. 50)

heat (hēt) The movement of energy from warmer to cooler objects. (p. 116)

GLOSSARY

PRONUNCIATION KEY

a at; ā ape; ä far; âr care; e end; ē me; i it; ī ice; îr pierce; o hot; ō old; ô fork; oi oil; ou out; u up; ū use; ü rule; ù pull; ûr turn; hw white; ng song; th thin; th this; zh measure; ə about, taken, pencil, lemon, circus

herbivore (hər′ bə vôr′) A consumer that eats only plants. (p. 56)

heredity (hə red′i tē) The passing of traits from parent to offspring. (p. 270)

hibernate (hī′bər nāt′) An instinct that causes some animals to sleep through the winter; all body processes slow down, and body temperature can drop to a few degrees above freezing. (p. 280)

horizon (hə rī′zən) A layer of soil differing from the layers above and below it. (p. 187)

humus (hū′məs) Leftover decomposed plant and animal matter in the soil. (p. 186)

I

ice cap (īs kap) A thick sheet of ice covering a large area of land. (p. 373)

igneous rock (ig′nē əs rok) "Fire-made" rock formed from melted rock material. (p. 151)

immovable joint (i mü′və bəl joint) A place where bones fit together too tightly to move. (p. 438)

imprint (n., im′print′) A fossil created by a print or impression. (p. 162)

inclined plane (in klīnd′ plān) A straight, slanted surface that is not moved when it is used. (p. 136)

inherited behavior (in her′i təd bi hāv′yər) A behavior that is inborn, not learned. (p. 280)

inner core (in′ər kôr) A sphere of solid material at Earth's center. (p. 202)

instinct (in′stingkt′) A pattern of behavior that requires no thinking because it is programmed into an animal's brain. (p. 280)

insulator (in′sə lā′tər) 1. A material that does not transfer heat very well. (p. 116) 2. Said of a material through which electricity does not flow easily. (p. 295)

invertebrate (in vûr′tə brit′) An animal without a backbone. (p. 214)

involuntary muscle (in vol′ən ter′ē mus′əl) A muscle that causes movements you cannot control. (p. 449)

irrigation (ir′i gā′shən) A way to get water into the soil by artificial means. (p. 422)

J

joint (joint) A place where two or more bones meet. (p. 438)

K

kidney (kid′nē) One of two main waste-removal organs in vertebrates that filters wastes from the blood. (p. 254)

kilogram (kil′ə gram′) The metric unit used to measure mass. (p. 70)

kingdom (king′dəm) One of the largest groups of organisms into which an organism can be classified. (p. 28)

L

larva (lär′və) A wormlike stage of some organisms that hatches from an egg during complete metamorphosis; a young organism with a form different from its parents. (p. 266)

lava (lä′və) Magma that reaches Earth's surface through volcanoes or cracks. (p. 151)

learned behavior (lûrnd bi hāv′yər) Behavior that is not inborn. (p. 281)

length (lengkth) The number of units that fit along one edge of something. (p. 80)

lever (lev′ər) A simple machine made of a rigid bar on a pivot point. (p. 132)

life cycle (līf sī′kəl) The stages of growth and change of an organism's life. (p. 266)

life span (līf span) How long an organism can be expected to live. (p. 267)

ligament (lig′ə mənt) A tough band of tissue that holds two bones together where they meet. (p. 439)

lightning (līt′ ning) A discharge of static electricity from a cloud to another cloud or to the ground. (p. 296)

liquid (lik′wid) A form of matter that takes up a definite amount of space and has no definite shape. (p. 71)

load (lōd) The object being lifted or moved. (p. 132)

LSD (el es dē) A mind-altering drug. (p. 473)

luster (lus′tər) The way a mineral reflects light. (p. 149)

M

magma (mag′mə) Melted rock material. (p. 151)

magnetic field (mag net′ik fēld) A region of magnetic force around a magnet. (p. 332)

mammal (mam′əl) A warm-blooded vertebrate with hair or fur that feeds milk to its young; most are born live. (p. 242)

mantle (man′təl) The layer of rock lying below the crust. (p. 202)

marijuana (mar′ə wä′nə) An illegal drug made from the crushed leaves, flowers, and seeds of the cannabis plant. (p. 473)

marrow (mar′ō) Soft tissue that fills some bones. (p. 437)

mass (mas) The amount of matter making up an object. (p. 70)

mass extinction (mas ek stingk′shən) The dying out at the same time of many different species. (p. 44)

matter (ma′tər) Anything that takes up space and has properties that you can observe and describe. (p. 68)

melt (melt) When water particles absorb heat energy and change from a solid to a liquid. (p. 387)

metamorphic rock (met′ə môr′fik rok) Rock whose form has been changed by heat and/or pressure. (p. 154)

metamorphosis (met′ə môr′fə sis) A process of changes during certain animals' development. (p. 264)

metric system (met′rik sis′təm) A system of measurement based on units of ten. (p. 80)

microorganism (mī′krō ôr′gə niz′əm) An organism that is so small you need a microscope to see it. (p. 8)

migrate (mī′grāt) An instinct that causes some animals to move to a different area to either avoid cold weather, find new food supplies, or find a safe place to breed and raise their young. (p. 280)

mimicry (mim′i krē) When one organism imitates the traits of another. (p. 278)

mineral (min′ər əl) A naturally occurring substance, neither plant nor animal. (p. 148)

misuse (*v.*, mis ūz′) To use a legal drug improperly or in an unsafe way. (p. 474)

mixture (miks′chər) Two or more types of matter that are mixed together and keep their own properties. (p. 92)

mold (mōld) *n.*, A fossil clearly showing the outside features of the organism. (p. 163)

mollusk (mol′əsk) A soft-bodied invertebrate. (p. 226)

molting (mōl′ting) A process by which an arthropod sheds its exoskeleton. (p. 228)

moraine (mə rān′) Rock debris carried and deposited as a glacier melts. (p. 177)

PRONUNCIATION KEY

a at; ā ape; ä far; âr care; e end; ē me; i it; ī ice; îr pierce; o hot; ō old; ô fork; oi oil; ou out; u up; ū use; ü rule; u̇ pull; ûr turn; hw white; ng song; th thin; <u>th</u> this; zh measure; ə about, taken, pencil, lemon, circus

GLOSSARY

movable joint (mü′və bəl joint) A place where bones meet and can move easily. (p. 438)

movable pulley (mü′və bəl pùl′ē) A pulley that increases the effort force needed to move an object. The pulley wheel can change position, but the direction of the force remains unchanged. *See* **pulley**. (p. 134)

muscular system (mus′kyə lər sis′təm) The organ system made up of muscles that move bones. (pp. 256, 449)

N

narcotic (när kot′ik) A type of medicine that is used as a painkiller. (p. 473)

nervous system (nûr′vəs sis′təm) The organ system that controls all other body systems. (p. 257)

newton (nü′tən) A metric unit for weight, measuring the amount of pull or push a force such as gravity produces between two masses. (p. 83)

nicotine (nik′ə tēn′) A poisonous, oily substance found in tobacco. (p. 462)

nucleus (nü′klē əs) A cell's central control station. (p. 15)

nymph (nimf) A stage of some organisms that hatch from an egg during incomplete metamorphosis; a nymph is a young insect that looks like an adult. (p. 267)

O

omnivore (om′ nə vôr′) A consumer that eats both animals and plants (p. 56)

open circuit (ō′pən sûr′kit) A broken or incomplete path that electricity cannot flow through. (p. 305)

order (ôr′dər) A smaller group within a class. Orders are made up of still smaller groups of similar organisms called *families*. (p. 30)

organ (ôr′gən) A group of tissues that work together to do a certain job. (p. 6)

organ system (ôr′gən sis′təm) A group of organs that work together to carry on life functions. (p. 6)

organism (ôr′gə niz′əm) A living thing that carries out five basic life functions on its own. (p. 4)

outer core (ou′tər kôr) A liquid layer of Earth lying below the mantle. (p. 202)

outwash plain (out′wôsh plān) Gravel, sand, and clay carried from glaciers by melting water and streams. (p. 179)

over-the-counter (ō′vər thə koun′tər) Said of a medicine that can be purchased off the shelves in stores. (p. 470)

oxygen (ok′sə jən) A part of the air that is needed by most organisms to live. (p. 4)

P

parallel circuit (par′ə lel′ sûr′kit) A circuit in which each energy-using device is connected to the cell separately. (p. 317)

partly immovable joint (pärt′lē i mü′və bəl joint) A place where bones meet and can move only a little. (p. 438)

passive smoke (pas′iv smōk) Smoke that is inhaled by someone other than the smoker. (p. 463)

penicillin (pen′ə sil′in) A type of antibiotic first developed from a type of mold. (p. 470)

periodic (pîr′ē od′ik) Repeating in a pattern, like the *periodic* table of the elements. (p. 90)

permeability (pûr′mē ə bil′i tē) The rate at which water can pass through a material. Water passes quickly through porous soils with a high permeability. (p. 191)

pesticide (pes′tə sīd′) A chemical that kills insects. (p. 423)

petrified (pet′rə fīd′) Said of parts of plants or animals, especially wood and bone, that have been preserved by being "turned to stone." (p. 165)

pharmacist (fär′mə sist) A person trained and licensed to prepare and give out medicines according to a doctor's orders. (p. 470)

phylum (fī′ləm), *pl.* **phyla** (fī′lə) A smaller group into which members of a kingdom are further classified. Members share at least one major characteristic, like having a backbone. (pp. 30, 222)

physical change (fiz′i kəl chānj) A change that begins and ends with the same type of matter. *See* **chemical change**. (p. 107)

plasma (plaz′mə) The liquid part of blood. (p. 252)

pole (pōl) One of two ends of a magnet; where a magnet's pull is strongest. (p. 330)

population (pop′yə lā′shən) One type of organism living in an area. (p. 50)

pore space (pôr spās) Any of the gaps between soil particles, usually filled with water and air. *Porous* soils have large, well-connected pore spaces. (pp. 190, 408)

precipitation (pri sip′i tā′shən) Water in the atmosphere that falls to Earth as rain, snow, hail, or sleet. (p. 386)

prescription (pri skrip′shən) An order from a doctor, usually for medicine. (p. 470)

producer (prə dü′sər) An organism, such as a plant, that makes food. (p. 54)

property (prop′ər tē) A characteristic of something that you can observe, such as mass, volume, weight, and density. (p. 68)

protective resemblance (prə tek′tiv ri zem′bləns) A type of adaptation in which an animal resembles something in its environment. (p. 276)

protist (prō′tist) Any of a variety of one-celled organisms that live in pond water. (p. 19)

pulley (pul′ē) A grooved wheel that turns by the action of a rope in the groove. *See* **fixed pulley** and **movable pulley**. (p. 134)

pupa (pū′pə) A stage of some organisms that follows the larva stage in complete metamorphosis; many changes take place as adult tissues and organs form. (p. 266)

R

radial symmetry (rā′dē əl sim′ə trē) A form of symmetry in which an animal has matching body parts that extend outward from a central point. (p. 215)

radiate (rā′dē āt′) To send energy traveling in all directions through space. (p. 354)

radiation (rā′dē ā′shən) The transfer of heat through space. (p. 119)

rechargeable battery (rē charj′ə bəl bat′ə rē) A battery in which the chemical reactions can be reversed by a recharger, allowing these batteries to be used again and again. (p. 357)

reflex (rē′fleks′) The simplest inherited behavior, which is automatic, like an animal scratching an itch. (p. 280)

regeneration (rē jen′ə rā′shən) A form of asexual reproduction in simple animals in which a whole animal develops from just a part of the original animal. (p. 268)

relative age (rel′ə tiv āj) The age of something compared to the age of another thing. (p. 153)

PRONUNCIATION KEY

a **at**; ā **ape**; ä **far**; âr **care**; e **end**; ē **me**; i **it**; ī **ice**; îr **pierce**; o **hot**; ō **old**; ô **fork**; oi **oil**; ou **out**; u **up**; ū **use**; ü **rule**; u **pull**; ûr **turn**; hw **white**; ng **song**; th **thin**; <u>th</u> **this**; zh **measure**; ə **about, taken, pencil, lemon, circus**

reptile (rep′təl) A cold-blooded vertebrate that lives on land and has a backbone, an endoskeleton, and waterproof skin with scales or plates. (p. 240)

resistor (ri zis′tər) A material through which electricity has difficulty flowing. (p. 307)

respiratory system (res′pər ə tôr′ē sis′təm) The organ system that brings oxygen to body cells and removes waste gas. (p. 253)

rock cycle (rok sī′kəl) A never-ending process by which rocks are changed from one type to another. (p. 155)

rock debris (rok də brē′) Boulders, rock fragments, gravel, sand, and soil that are picked up by a glacier as it moves. (p. 176)

runoff (run′ôf′) The water that flows over Earth's surface but does not evaporate or soak into the ground. (p. 409)

S

scale (skāl) An instrument used to measure weight. (p. 83)

screw (skrü) An inclined plane that is wrapped around a pole. (p. 137)

sediment (sed′ə mənt) Deposited rock particles and other materials that settle in a liquid. (p. 152)

sedimentary rock (sed′ə men′tə rē rok) Rock formed from bits or layers of rocks cemented together. (p. 152)

seismic wave (sīz′mik wāv) A vibration caused by rocks moving and breaking along faults. (p. 200)

seismogram (sīz′mə gram′) The record of seismic waves made by a seismograph. (p. 201)

seismograph (sīz′mə graf′) An instrument that detects, measures, and records the energy of earthquake vibrations. (p. 198)

septic tank (sep′tik tangk) An underground tank in which sewage is broken down by bacteria. (p. 425)

series circuit (sîr′ēz sûr′kit) A circuit in which the current must flow through one energy-using device in order to flow through the other. (p. 316)

sewage (sü′ij) Water mixed with waste. (p. 425)

sewer (sü′ər) A large pipe or channel that carries sewage to a sewage treatment plant. (p. 425)

sexual reproduction (sek′shü əl rē′prə duk′shən) Producing offspring with two parents. (p. 268)

short circuit (shôrt sûr′kit) When too much current flows through a conductor. (p. 308)

side effect (sīd i fekt′) An unwanted result of using a medicine. (p. 471)

simple machine (sim′pəl mə shēn′) A machine with few moving parts that makes it easier to do work. (p. 130)

skeletal muscle (skel′i təl mus′əl) A muscle that is attached to a bone and allows movement. (p. 446)

skeletal system (skel′i təl sis′təm) The organ system made up of bones, cartilage, and ligaments. (pp. 256, 439)

skeleton (skel′i tən) An internal supporting frame that gives the body its shape and protects many organs. (p. 436)

smooth muscle (smüth mus′əl) The type of muscle that makes up internal organs and blood vessels. (p. 449)

soil profile (soil prō′fil) A vertical section of soil from the surface down to bedrock. (p. 187)

soil water (soil wô′tər) Water that soaks into the ground. (p. 374)

solid (sol'id) A form of matter that has a definite shape and takes up a definite amount of space. (p. 70)

species (spē'shēz) The smallest classification group, made up of only one type of organism that can reproduce with others of the same species; for example, all dogs belong to the same species. (p. 30)

sperm (spûrm) The male sex cell. (p. 269)

spherical symmetry (sfer'i kəl sim'ə trē) A form of symmetry in which the parts of an animal with a round body match up when it is folded through its center. (p. 215)

sponge (spunj) The simplest kind of invertebrate. (p. 214)

sprain (sprān) A pull or tear in a muscle or ligament. (p. 439)

standard unit (stan'dərd ū'nit) A unit of measure that people all understand and agree to use. (p. 80)

state (stāt) A form of matter, such as a solid, liquid, or gas; how quickly the particles of matter vibrate, how much heat energy they have, and how they are arranged determine the state of matter. (p. 70)

static electricity (stat'ik i lek tris'i tē) A buildup of an electrical charge. (p. 294)

stimulant (stim'yə lənt) A substance that speeds up the activity of the body. (p. 462)

streak plate (strēk plāt) A glass plate that a mineral can be rubbed against to find out the color of the streak it leaves. (p. 149)

subsoil (sub'soil') A hard layer of clay and minerals that lies beneath topsoil. (p. 187)

surface current (sûr'fis kûr'ənt) The movement of the ocean caused by steady winds blowing over the ocean. (p. 397)

switch (swich) A device that can open or close an electric circuit. (p. 309)

symmetry (sim'ə trē) The way an animal's body parts match up around a point or central line. (p. 214)

system (sis'təm) A group of parts that work together. (p. 6)

T

tar (tär) A sticky, brown substance found in tobacco. (p. 462)

temperature (tem'pər ə chər) A measure of how hot or cold something is. (p. 121)

tendon (ten'dən) A strong band of tissue that connects a muscle to bone. (p. 447)

terminal (tûr'mə nəl) One of two places where wires can be attached to a cell or battery. (p. 306)

terminus (tûr'mə nəs) The end, or outer margin, of a glacier where rock debris accumulates. (p. 177)

thermometer (thər mom'i tər) An instrument used to measure temperature. (p. 121)

tide (tīd) The rise and fall of ocean water levels. (p. 398)

tissue (tish'ü) A group of similar cells that work together to carry out a job. (p. 5)

topsoil (top'soil') The dark, top layer of soil, rich in humus and minerals, in which many tiny organisms live and most plants grow. (p. 187)

trait (trāt) A characteristic of an organism. (p. 28)

tranquilizer (trang'kwə lī'zər) A type of medicine used to calm a person. (p. 472)

PRONUNCIATION KEY

a **at**; ā **ape**; ä **far**; âr **care**; e **end**; ē **me**; i **it**; ī **ice**; îr **pierce**; o **hot**; ō **old**; ô **fork**; oi **oil**; ou **out**; u **up**; ū **use**; ü **rule**; u̇ **pull**; ûr **turn**; hw **white**; ng **song**; th **thin**; <u>th</u> **this**; zh **measure**; ə **about, taken, pencil, lemon, circus**

transformer (trans fôr′mər) A device in which alternating current in one coil produces current in a second coil. (p. 346)

transpiration (tran′spə rā′shən) The process whereby plants release water vapor into the air through their leaves. (p. 411)

triceps (trī′seps) A muscle on the outside of the upper arm that straightens the arm by contracting. (p. 446)

U

urine (yùr′in) The concentrated wastes filtered by the kidneys. (p. 254)

V

vacuole (vak′ū ōl′) A holding bin for food, water, and waste. (p. 15)

vertebrate (vûr′tə brāt′) An animal with a backbone. (p. 214)

virus (vī′rəs) Nonliving particles smaller than cells that are able to reproduce inside living cells. (p. 20)

volt (vōlt) A unit for measuring the force that makes negative charges flow. (p. 345)

volume (vol′ūm) How much space an object takes up. (p. 81)

voluntary muscle (vol′ən ter′ē mus′əl) A muscle that causes movements you can control. (p. 449)

W

warm-blooded (wôrm′blud′id) Said of an animal with a constant body temperature. (p. 236)

water conservation (wôtər kon′sər vā′shən) The use of water-saving methods. (p. 426)

water cycle (wô′tər sī′kəl) The continuous movement of water between Earth's surface and the air, changing from liquid to gas to liquid. (p. 388)

water table (wô′tər tā′bəl) The upper area of groundwater. (p. 408)

water treatment plant (wô′tər trēt′mənt plant) A place where water is made clean and pure. (p. 424)

water vapor (wô′tər vā′pər) Water as a gas in Earth's atmosphere. (p. 372)

wave (wāv) An up-and-down movement of water. (p. 399)

weathering (weth′ər ing) The process of breaking down rocks into smaller pieces that create sediment. (p. 155)

wedge (wej) A simple machine made by combining two inclined planes. It translates a downward force into two outward forces in opposite directions. (p. 137)

weight (wāt) The measure of the pull of gravity between an object and Earth. (p. 83)

wet cell (wet sel) A device that produces electricity using two different metal bars placed in an acid solution. (p. 344)

wheel and axle (hwēl and ak′səl) A simple machine made of a handle or axis attached to the center of a wheel. (p. 135)

work (wûrk) To apply a force that makes an object move. An object must move some distance to call what happens work. (p. 128)

INDEX

*Indicates an activity related to this topic.

INDEX

*Indicates an activity related to this topic.

W

*Indicates an activity related to this topic.

CREDITS

Design & Production: Kirchoff/Wohlberg, Inc.

Maps: Geosystems.

Transvision: Stephen Ogilvy (photography); Guy Porfirio (illustration).

Illustrations: Kenneth Batelman: pp. 74, 105, 121; Dan Brown: pp. 376, 384, 385, 388-389, 389, 398, 399, 400, 408, 410; Elizabeth Callen: pp. 284, 368; Barbara Cousins: pp. 252, 253, 254, 255, 256, 257, 266; Steven Cowden: pp. 296, 297, 298, 318-319, 348, 354; Michael DiGiorgio: pp. 56, 58, 215, 222, 236; Jeff Fagan: pp. 132, 133, 137; Howard S. Friedman: p. 54; Colin Hayes: pp. 127, 134, 135, 310, 333, 343, 346, 347, 445, R7, R11, R13, R15, R20-R23; Tom Leonard: pp. 4, 5, 6, 16, 42, 43, 44, 51, 213, 225, 237, 264, 265, 268, 271, 332, 335, 344, 356, 362, 370, 436, 437, 438, 446, 447, 448, 449, 459; Olivia: pp. 24, 61, 64, 100, 141, 172, 205, 248, 285, 294, 326, 365, 404, 429, 454, 477, R2-R4, R9, R10, R13, R16-R19, R23-R25; Sharron O'Neil: pp. 14, 15, 20, 28, 31, 40, 41, 153, 176, 186, 190, 191, 374, 411; Vilma Ortiz-Dillon: pp. 144, 208, 386, 396, 397, 421, 424, 425, 432; Rob Schuster: pp. 84, 108, 117, 118, 120, 179, 307, 322, 342, 355, 358, 359; Matt Straub: pp. 7, 33, 243, 458, 461, 480; Ted Williams: pp. 69, 92, 93, 95, 119, 154, 155, 198, 200, 201, 202, 338-339, 392-393, 456, 457, 463, 465, 469; Craig Zolman: pp. 303, 304, 305, 306, 308, 309, 316, 317, 318, 319, 320, 321, 368.

Photography Credits:

Contents: iii: Jim Battles/Debinsky Photo Associates. iv: inset, Corbis; Richard Price/FPG. v: E.R. Degginger/Bruce Coleman, Inc. vi: R. Williams/Bruce Coleman, Inc. vii: Jim Foster/The Stock Market. viii: Steve Wilkings/The Stock Market. ix: Mehau Kulyk/Science Photo Library.

National Geographic Invitation to Science: S2: t. Michael Nichols/National Geographic; b. Vanne Goodall. S3: t., b. Michael Nichols/National Geographic.

Be a Scientist: S4: bkgrd. Paul S. Howell/Liaison Agency; inset, Stuart Westmorland/Tony Stone Images. S5: David Mager. S6: t. Steven M. Barnett; m. The Granger Collection, New York; b. Corbis. S7: t. Bruce Avera Hunter/National Geographic Society-Image Collection; b. Michael Justice/Liaison. S8: Eric Neurath/Stock, Boston. S10: Robert Halstead-TPI/Masterfile. S11: l. Stuart Westmorland/Tony Stone Images; r. Steinhart Aquarium/Tom McHugh/Photo Researchers, Inc. S12: James Stanfield. S13: l. Tom Tracy/Tony Stone Images; c. Steven M. Barnett; r. Andrew Wood/Photo Researchers, Inc. S14: The Granger Collection, New York. S15: t. National Geographic Society Photographic Laboratory; b. David Mager. S16: t., b. David Doubilet. S17: Jeff Rotman/Tony Stone Images. S19: Stephen Ogilvy.

Unit 1: 1: F.C. Millington/TCL Masterfile; John Lythgoe/TCL Masterfile. 2: Stephen Ogilvy. 3: t., b. Stephen Ogilvy. 7: Stephen Ogilvy. 8: l. David M. Philipps/Photo Researchers, Inc.; r. Astrid & Hanns-Frieder/Photo Researchers, Inc.; b.l. Michael Abbey/Photo Researchers, Inc.; b.r. Edward R. Degginger/Bruce Coleman, Inc. 9: Ann & Carl Purcell/Words & Pictures/PNI. 10: l. Enrico Ferorelli; r. Phyllis Picardi/Stock, Boston/PNI. 11: Dan McCoy/Rainbow/PNI. 12: Stephen Ogilvy. 13: Nigel Cattlin/Photo Researchers, Inc. 17: Stephen Ogilvy. 18: l. & r. PhotoDisc; inset t.l. & inset t.r. Biophoto Associates/Photo Researchers, Inc.; inset b.l. Ken Edward/Photo Researchers, Inc.; inset b.r. J.F. Gennaro/Photo Researchers, Inc. 19: t.l. M.I. Walker/Photo Researchers, Inc.; m.l. Biophoto Associates/Photo Researchers, Inc.; b.l. Eric V. Grave/Photo Researchers, Inc.; inset r. CNRI/Science Photo/Photo Researchers, Inc.; r. Joy Spur/Bruce Coleman, Inc. 21: Doctor Dennis Kunkel/Phototake/PNI. 22-23: David Scharf/Peter Arnold, Inc. 23: R. Maisonneuve/Photo Researchers, Inc.; V.I. LAB E.R.I.C./FPG. 25: Tom & Pat Leeson. 26: Stephen Ogilvy. 27: t.l. Gregory Ochocki/Photo Researchers, Inc.; t.r. J. Foott/Tom Stack & Associates; m.l. Charlie Heidecker/Visuals Unlimited; m.r. Carl R. Sams II/Peter Arnold, Inc.; b.l. Hans Pfletschinger/Peter Arnold, Inc.; b.r. Mike Bacon/Tom Stack & Associates. 29: M.I. Walker/Photo Researchers, Inc. 30: Margaret Miller/Photo Researchers, Inc. 32: Stephen Ogilvy. 33: PhotoDisc. 34: l. Richard R. Hansen/Photo Researchers, Inc.; r. Jany Sauvanet/Photo Researchers, Inc.; b. Kevin Schafer/Corbis. 35: l. Adam Jones/Photo Researchers, Inc.; m. Stephen Dalton/Photo Researchers, Inc.; r. Scott Camazine/Photo Researchers, Inc. 36: Dieter & Mary Plage/Bruce Coleman, Inc. 37: Edward R. Degginger/Bruce Coleman, Inc. 38: Francois Gohier/Photo Researchers, Inc. 39: l. Biophoto Associates/Photo Researchers, Inc.; r. Edward R. Degginger/Photo Researchers, Inc. 41: Stephen Ogilvy. 43: Charles E. Mohr/Photo Researchers, Inc. 45: Tom McHugh/Photo Researchers, Inc. 46: Project Lokahi. 46-47: Ken Lucas/Visuals Unlimited. 48: Stephen J. Krasemann/Photo Researchers, Inc. 49: Stephen Ogilvy. 50: Stephen Ogilvy. 51: Stephen Ogilvy. 52: l. Stephen Krasemann/Photo Researchers, Inc.; m. Jim Steinberg/Photo Researchers, Inc.; r. Renee Lynn/Photo Researchers, Inc. 53: b.l. C.K. Lorenz/Photo Researchers, Inc.; m. Leonide Principe/Photo Researchers, Inc.; r. F. Stuart Westmorland/Photo Researchers, Inc. 55: t. Microfield Scientific/Photo Researchers, Inc.; b. Andrew J. Martinez/Photo Researchers, Inc. 56: inset, Charlie Ott/Photo Researchers, Inc. 56-57: Stephen Dalton/Photo Researchers, Inc. 57: r. Stephen Ogilvy. 59: Arthur Tilley/FPG. 60: Chinch Gryniewicz/Ecoscene/Corbis.

Unit 2: 65: Picture Perfect; Phil Degginger/Bruce Coleman, Inc. 66: PhotoDisc. 67: Stephen Ogilvy. 68: Stephen Ogilvy. 70: Stephen Ogilvy. 71: r. PhotoDisc; l. Stephen Ogilvy. 72: r. Charles Gupton/AllStock/PNI; l. Stephen Ogilvy. 73: all Stephen Ogilvy. 74: Stephen Ogilvy. 75: Stephen Ogilvy. 76: l. James A. Sugar/Black Star/PNI; r. Lisa Quinones/Black Star/PNI. 77: James A. Sugar/Black Star/PNI. 78: Stephen Ogilvy. 79: Stephen Ogilvy. 80: PhotoDisc. 82: Stephen Ogilvy. 83: Stephen Ogilvy. 84: Stephen Ogilvy. 85: Craig Tuttle/The Stock Market. 86: Stephen Ogilvy. 87: t. BIPM; b. Stockbyte. 88: PhotoDisc. 89: Stephen Ogilvy. 91: Corbis/Bettmann. 92: Stephen Ogilvy. 94: Stephen Ogilvy. 95: Stephen Ogilvy. 96: PhotoDisc; (soda can) Steven Needham/Envision. 97: Stephen Ogilvy. 98: t. Science Photo Library/Photo Researchers. 98-99: b. Chris Collins/The Stock Market. 99: Corbis/Bettmann. 101: Stock Imagery, Inc.; E.J. West/Stock Imagery, Inc. 102: l. Jean Higgins/Envision; r. Rafael Macia/Photo Researchers, Inc. 103: Stephen Ogilvy. 104: col 1: l. Michael Keller/FPG; r. Charles Winters/Photo Researchers, Inc.; col 2: t. Ron Rovtar/FPG; b. James L. Amos/Photo Researchers, Inc. 106: l. Stephen Ogilvy; r.t. R.B. Smith/Dembinsky Photo; r.b. Charles Winters/Photo Researchers, Inc. 109: Stephen Ogilvy. 110: col 1: t. Gerald Zanetti/The Stock Market; m. Biophoto Associates/Photo Researchers, Inc.; b. Philip James Corwin/Corbis; col 2: t. Robert Jonathan Kligge/The Stock Market; m. Brownie Harris/The Stock Market; b. Adam Hart-Davis/Photo Researchers, Inc.; 111: Stephen Ogilvy. 112: t. Joel Arrington/Visuals Unlimited; m. David McGlynn/FPG; b. Paul Bierman/Visuals Unlimited. 112-113: PhotoDisc. 113: Sylvan Wittwer/Visuals Unlimited. 114: Richard Ellis/Photo Researchers, Inc. 115: Stephen Ogilvy. 116: Stephen Ogilvy. 117: Stephen Ogilvy. 119: Stephen Ogilvy. 122: t. Edward R. Degginger/Bruce Coleman, Inc.; m. Tim Davis/Photo Researchers, Inc.; b. Hans Reinhard/Bruce Coleman, Inc. 124: PhotoDisc; Ken Karp. 125: Jade Albert/FPG. 126: Debra P. Hershkowitz. 128: l. Idaho Ketchum/The Stock Market; r. Dollarhide Monkmeyer. 129: Hank Morgan/Photo Researchers, Inc. 130: l. Steve Elmore/Bruce Coleman, Inc.; b. Edward R. Degginger/Bruce Coleman, Inc.; r. J. Fennell/Bruce Coleman, Inc. 131: l. Tony Freeman/PhotoEdit; c. Kenneth H. Thomas/Photo Researchers, Inc.; t.r. Tony Freeman/PhotoEdit; b.r. Science VU/Visuals Unlimited. 133: David Mager. 135: Alan Schein/The Stock Market. 136: David Young-Wolff/PhotoEdit. 138: Michal Newman/PhotoEdit. 139: PhotoDisc. 140: l. Culver Pictures, Inc.; m. www.artoday.com.

Unit 3: 145: Carr Clifton; Tom Bean. 146: Sinclair Stammers/Photo Researchers, Inc. 147: Stephen Ogilvy. 148: l.&m.r. Ken Karp; m.l. ©Tom Pantages/Photo Take; r. Stephen Ogilvy; b. Joyce Photographics/Photo Researchers, Inc. 149: t.r. Corbis; t.l. Stephen Ogilvy; b.r. A.J. Copley/VU; b.l. Mark A. Schneider/VU. 150: PhotoDisc. 151: l. Stephen Ogilvy; m.&r. E.R. Degginger/Photo Researchers, Inc. 152: t.l. Charles Winters/Photo Researchers, Inc.; t.r. Ken Karp; b.l. ©Martin G. Miller/VU; b.r. Andrew J. Martinez/Photo Researchers, Inc. 153: Stephen Ogilvy. 154: Corbis. 156: t. J C Carton/Bruce Coleman, Inc.; b. Edward R. Degginger/Bruce Coleman, Inc. 157: Stephen Ogilvy. 158: t. David Burnett/Contract Press Images/PNI; b. E.R. Degginger/Photo Researchers, Inc. 159: NASA. 160: l. Weststock; m. PhotoDisc. 162: Francois Gohier/Photo Researchers, Inc.; 163: l. Charles R. Belinky/Photo Researchers, Inc.; r. Stephen Ogilvy. 164: l. Edward R. Degginger/Bruce Coleman, Inc.; r. Novosti/Photo Researchers, Inc. 165: l. A.J. Copley/Visuals Unlimited; r. Ed Bohon/The Stock Market. 166: Carlos Goldin/Photo Researchers, Inc. 167: A.J. Copley/Visuals Unlimited. 168: l. Tom McHugh/Photo Researchers, Inc.; r. A.J. Copley/Visuals Unlimited. 169: l. Phototake/PNI; r. Phil Degginger/Bruce Coleman, Inc. 170: Richard Lydekker/Linda Hall Library. 171: courtesy Lisa White. 173: N.&M. Freeman/Bruce Coleman, Inc. 174: Lee Foster/Bruce Coleman, Inc. 175: Stephen Ogilvy. 177: Charlie

Heidecker/Visuals Unlimited. 178: Ken Cavanagh. 180: John Serrao/Photo Researchers, Inc. 181: Joyce Photographics/Photo Researchers, Inc. 182-183: Ron Sanford/The Stock Market. 183: Photo Researchers, Inc. 184: Stephen Ogilvy. 185: Stephen Ogilvy. 187: Black/Bruce Coleman, Inc. 188: Stephen Ogilvy. 188-189: Janis Burger/Bruce Coleman, Inc. 190: Stephen Ogilvy. 192: Kazuyoshi Nomachi/Photo Researchers, Inc. 193: Richard T. Nowitz/Photo Researchers, Inc. 195: t.r. Barry Hennings/Photo Researchers, Inc.; b.l. Franco Sal-Moiragni/The Stock Market; t.l. Gary S. Withey/Bruce Coleman, Inc.; bkgrd. Lynette Cook/Science Photo Library/Photo Researchers, Inc. 196: Stephen Ogilvy. 197: Stephen Ogilvy. 199: l. PhotoDisc; r. Stephen Ogilvy. 203: Russell D. Curtis/Photo Researchers, Inc. 204: Corbis.

Unit 4: 209: Art Wolf/Tony Stone Images. 210: Hans Reinhard/Bruce Coleman, Inc. 211: Stephen Ogilvy. 212: l. Maryann Frazier/Photo Researchers, Inc.; r. Scott Smith/Animals Animals. 214: l. Stephen Ogilvy; r. Charles V. Angelo/Photo Researchers, Inc. 216: t.r. Joe McDonald/Bruce Coleman, Inc.; m.r. James R. McCullagh/Visuals Unlimited; b.l. Neil S. McDaniel/Photo Researchers, Inc.; b.c. Ron & Valerie Taylor/Bruce Coleman, Inc.; b.r. John Chellman/Animals Animals. 217: l. David Doubilet; r. Andrew J. Martinez/Photo Researchers, Inc. 218: Sisse Brimberg/National Geographic Image Collection. 219: t. Fran Coleman/Animals Animals; b. Joel Sartore. 220: l. & r. Chip Clark. 221: t. Kim Taylor/Bruce Coleman, Inc; b. Ray Coleman/Photo Researchers, Inc. 223: inset, Marian Bacon/Animals Animals; t. Sefton/Bruce Coleman, Inc. 224: t. Carol Geake/Animals Animals; b. J.H. Robinson/Photo Researchers, Inc. 226: l. Joyce & Frank Burek/Animals Animals; b.r. Zig Leszcynski/Animals Animals. 227: Doug Sokell/Visuals Unlimited. 228: l. Jane Burton/Bruce Coleman, Inc.; r. Tom McHugh/Photo Researchers, Inc. 229: col 1: L. West/Photo Researchers, Inc.; insets l. & r. Dwight Kuhn; col 2 clockwise from top: L. West/Bruce Coleman, Inc.; John D. Cunningham/Visuals Unlimited; Mary Beth Angelo/Photo Researchers, Inc.; Cabisco/Visuals Unlimited; Fabio Colombini/Animals Animals; Mary Snyderman/Visuals Unlimited. 230-231: L. Newman A./Photo Researchers, Inc. 231: William J. Pohley/Visuals Unlimited. 232: t.l. Richard Hamilton Smith/Dembinsky Photo Assoc. 232-233: PhotoDisc. 233: t. Richard T. Nowitz/Photo Researchers,Inc.; David Young-Wolf/PhotoEdit. 234: Stephen Ogilvy. 235: Norman Owen Tomalin/Bruce Coleman, Inc. 237: Hans Reinhard/Bruce Coleman, Inc. 238: Dave B. Fleetham/Visuals Unlimited; inset, Jane Burton/Bruce Coleman, Inc. 239: t. G.I. Bernard/OSF Animals Animals; b. L. West/Bruce Coleman, Inc. 240: Tom McHugh/Photo Researchers, Inc. 241: Roy David Farris/Visuals Unlimited. 242: Jean Phillipe Varin/Photo Researchers, Inc. 243: clockwise from t.l.: Dan Guravich/Photo Researchers, Inc.; Ron & Valerie Taylor/Bruce Coleman, Inc.; Jeff Lepore/Photo Researchers, Inc.; Dwight R. Kuhn; Wally Eberhart/Visuals Unlimited; Zig Leszczynski/Animals Animals. 244: Stephen Ogilvy. 245: t. Eric & David Hosking/Corbis; b. W. Perry Conway/Corbis. 246: Douglas Faulkner/Photo Researchers, Inc. 247: inset, Kennan Ward/Bruce Coleman, Inc.; bkgrd. Peter B. Kaplan/Photo Researchers, Inc. 249: Charles Krebs/Tony Stone Images; L.L. Rue III/Bruce Coleman, Inc. 250: PhotoDisc. 251: Stephen Ogilvy. 258: Kjell B. Sandved/Photo Researchers, Inc. 259: Stephen Spotte/Photo Researchers, Inc. 260: PhotoDisc. 261: b.r. PhotoDisc; t.l. Larry Cameron/Photo Researchers, Inc.; t.r. Norman Owen Tomalin/Bruce Coleman, Inc. 262: Gerard Lacz/Animals Animals. 263: Stephen Ogilvy. 270: Stephen Ogilvy. 271: AP/Wide World Photos. 272: Stephen Ogilvy. 273: b.r. D. Long/Visuals Unlimited; bkgrd. G. Buttner/Okapia/Photo Researchers, Inc.; r. Wally Eberhart/Visuals Unlimited. 274: Michael Fogden/Bruce Coleman, Inc. 276: Breck P. Kent/Animals Animals; Michael Fogden/Bruce Coleman, Inc. 277: K & K Ammann/Bruce Coleman, Inc. 278: John Shaw/Bruce Coleman, Inc. 280: l. Maria Zorn/Animals Animals; r. W.J.C. Murray/Bruce Coleman, Inc. 282: Rita Nannini/Photo Researchers, Inc. 283: A. Ramey/PhotoEdit. 284: PhotoDisc; b.r. Thomas C. Boyden/Dembinsky Photo Assoc.

Unit 5: 289: PhotoDisc. 290: Tim Davis/Photo Researchers, Inc. 291: Stephen Ogilvy. 292: Stockbyte. 293: PhotoDisc. 294: PhotoDisc. 295: Stephen Ogilvy. 297: Kent Wood/Photo Researchers, Inc. 299: PhotoDisc. 300: l. The Granger Collection, New York; r. Dale Camera Graphics/Phototake/PNI. 301: The Granger Collection, New York. 302: Stephen Ogilvy. 305: Stephen Ogilvy. 308: Stephen Ogilvy. 309: Norbert Wu. 311: Stephen Ogilvy. 312: b.l. Culver Pictures, Inc.; m. Stock Montage, Inc.; b.r. PhotoDisc; t.r. Rich Treptow/Photo Researchers, Inc. 313: m. Norman Owen Tomalin/Bruce Coleman, Inc.; b.r. Will & Deni McIntyre/Photo Researchers, Inc. 314: PhotoDisc. 315: Stephen Ogilvy. 322: l. PhotoDisc; r. Norman Owen Tomalin/Bruce Coleman, Inc. 323: Stephen Ogilvy. 324: Don Mason/The Stock Market. 324-325: Michael W. Davidson/Photo Researchers, Inc. 325: David Parker/Seagate/Photo Researchers, Inc. 327: PhotoDisc. 328: Stephen Ogilvy. 329: Stephen Ogilvy. 330: Stephen Ogilvy. 331: Stephen Ogilvy. 332: Stephen Ogilvy.

334: l. Stephen Ogilvy; r. David R. Frazier/Photo Researchers, Inc. 336: l. Stephen Ogilvy; r. Science Photo Library/Photo Researchers, Inc. 337: Stephen Ogilvy. 340: AP/Wide World Photos. 341: Stephen Ogilvy. 345: Stephen Ogilvy. 346: Ken Sherman/Bruce Coleman, Inc. 349: Historical Picture Archive/Corbis. 350: Stephen Ogilvy. 351: t. Elena Rooraid/PhotoEdit; b. Dennis Hallinan/FPG. 352: Stephen Ogilvy. 353: Stephen Ogilvy. 355: Stephen Ogilvy. 357: Stephen Ogilvy. 358: Stephen Ogilvy. 359: Stephen Ogilvy. 360: l. Martin Withers/Dembinsky Photo & PhotoDisc; c. Gelfan/Monkmeyer; r. Andrew/Photo Researchers, Inc. 360-361: PhotoDisc. 361: l. Charles D. Winters/Photo Researchers, Inc.; b. Stockbyte; r. Aaron Haupt/Photo Researchers, Inc. 363: Stephen Ogilvy. 364: bkgrd. Arthur Tilley/FPG; b.l. Robert Pettit/Dembinsky Photo; t.r. Schneider Studio/The Stock Market; b.r. Simon Fraser/Photo Researchers, Inc.; t.l. Werner Bertsch/Bruce Coleman, Inc.

Unit 6: 369: Picture Perfect; John Turner/Tony Stone Images. 371: Stephen Ogilvy. 372: Planet Earth Pictures/FPG. 373: l. PhotoDisc; r. Courtesy of Lake Michigan. 374: Roy Morsch/The Stock Market. 375: Joe McDonald/Bruce Coleman, Inc.; inset, Ron & Valerie Taylor. 377: Stephen Ogilvy. 378: Stephen Ogilvy. 379: Wendell Metzen/Bruce Coleman, Inc. 380-381: L.A. Frank, The University of Iowa & NASA/Goddard Space Flight Center; Michael Freeman/Bruce Coleman, Inc./PNI; Chad Ehlers/Photo Network/PNI. 382: Stephen Ogilvy. 383: Stephen Ogilvy. 386: Stephen Ogilvy. 387: inset, Joe DiMaggio/The Stock Market; Lee Rentz/Bruce Coleman, Inc. 390: t. John Shaw/Bruce Coleman, Inc.; b. Howard B. Bluestein/Photo Researchers, Inc. 391: Steve Smith/FPG. 392: Library of Congress/Corbis. 393: l. Barry L. Runk/Grant Heilman; r. Charles D. Winters/Photo Researchers, Inc. 394: Stephen Ogilvy. 395: Stephen Ogilvy. 398: t. & b. Andrew J. Martinez/Photo Researchers, Inc. 399: Stephen Ogilvy. 401: bkgrd. & inset, Courtesy of Bruce M. Richmond/USGS. 402: Wendell Metzen/Bruce Coleman, Inc. 403: bkgrd. PhotoDisc; b. Gary Randall/ FPG; m. Martin Bond/Science Photo Library/Photo Researchers, Inc. 405: Superstock; Chris Vincent/The Stock Market. 406: Culver Pictures, Inc. 407: Stephen Ogilvy. 409: l. Michael S. Renner/Bruce Coleman, Inc.; r. Stephen Ogilvy. 412: l. PhotoDisc; inset, J. Dermid/Bruce Coleman, Inc. 413: Richard & Susan Day/Animals Animals. 414: Stephen Ogilvy. 415: PhotoDisc. 416: l. Corbis/Bettmann; r. AP/Wide World Photos. 416-417: Black/Bruce Coleman, Inc. 417: t.l. AP/Wide World Photos; t.r. Corbis/UPI/Bettman; b. AP/Wide World Photos. 418: PhotoDisc. 419: Stephen Ogilvy. 420: PhotoDisc. 421: Richard Hutchings/Photo Researchers, Inc. 422: all PhotoDisc. 423: b. PhotoDisc; r. Blackstone R. Millbury/Bruce Coleman, Inc. 425: Norman Owen Tomalin/Bruce Coleman, Inc. 426: John Elk III/Bruce Coleman, Inc. 427: Stephen Ogilvy. 428: m. David L. Pearson/Visuals Unlimited; bkgrd. John Shaw/Bruce Coleman; t. John Gerlach/Dembinsky Photo Assoc.

Unit 7: 433: Ken Chernus/FPG; J.Y. Mallet/PhotoEdit. 434: Adam Jones/Dembinsky Photo. 435: Stephen Ogilvy. 439: Stephen Ogilvy. 441: Stephen Ogilvy. 442: l. Billy E. Barnes/PhotoEdit/PNI; r. Dept. of Clinical Radiology, Salisbury District Hospital/SPL/Photo Researchers, Inc. 444: Michael Krasowitz/FPG. 446: Dwight R. Kuhn. 447: l. & c. Stephen Ogilvy; r. Rob Curtis/VIREO. 448: CNRI/Photo Researchers, Inc. 449: Marshall Sklar/Photo Researchers, Inc. 450: Stephen Ogilvy. 451: Stephen Ogilvy. 452: b. Corbis; t. Mark E. Gibson/Dembinsky Photo. 453: t. Blair Seitz/Photo Researchers, Inc.; b. Mark Gibson/Visuals Unlimited. 455: Bill Losh/FPG. 458: Michael A. Keller/The Stock Market. 460: Stephen Ogilvy. 462: Matt Meadows/Peter Arnold, Inc. 463: Arthur Tilley/FPG. 466: PhotoDisc. 467: Mark C. Burnett/ Photo Researchers, Inc. 468: Stephen Ogilvy. 470: José Pelaez/The Stock Market. 473: Bill Beatty/Visuals Unlimited. 474: l. Stephen Ogilvy; r. Jeff Greenberg/PhotoEdit. 476: m. Barros & Barros/The Image Bank; t. Bill Bachmann/Photo Researchers, Inc.; bkgrd. Ed Gallucci/The Stock Market.

Handbook: Steven Ogilvy: pp. R6, R8, R12, R14, R15, R26.